AF345837

THE
KNOWLEDGE
OF WISDOM

THE KNOWLEDGE OF WISDOM

Walking in the Light of Divine Peace, Prosperity and Security

JEROHAM C. IBEH

Gushing Stream Publications Ltd

Copyright © 2020 by Jeroham C. Ibeh

The Knowledge of Wisdom

Published by Gushing Stream Publications Ltd
Lagos - Nigeria
gushingstreampublications@gmail.com

First Printing, 2020

Printed in the United States of America

ISBN 978-2-9574303-0-7

All rights reserved. No part of this book may be repro-
duced in any manner whatsoever without written per-
mission except in the case of brief quotations
embodied in critical articles and reviews.

Unless otherwise indicated, Scripture quotations are
from the King James Version of the Bible. Copyright ©
1994 by Zondervan.

Contents

INTRODUCTION

ABOUT THE AUTHOR

BY JEROHAM C. IBEH

Introduction

You cannot avert a prophetic agenda; you can only seek an exemption. Until Jesus returns, there will always be a global economic crash, political crisis, wars, outbreaks of viruses, killings, bombings, earthquakes, etc. You cannot stop any of THESE from happening, but you can seek an exemption for yourself and your loved ones.

*Oh how great is thy goodness, which thou hast laid up for them that fear thee; which thou hast wrought for them that trust in thee before the sons of men! Thou shalt hide them in the secret of thy presence from the **pride of man**: thou shalt keep them secretly in a pavilion from **the strife of tongues**. (Psalm 31:19-20).*

Again, until Jesus returns, the pride of man will continue to threaten the economic, health, and social lives of the human race. The pride of man in politics will continue to rule instead of to *lead*.

The pride of man in the financial services industry will continue to cause and finance wars among nations so that they can afterward gain control of the defeated country by installing a puppet government and then subject its citizens to abject poverty while looting the gold and diamond, oil, and other mineral resources beneath its soil. *Divide and rule!*

Or, are we talking about nations whose citizens have been miss-educated, and through that miss-education, they are deprived of the knowledge to utilize and produce from what they have beneath their soil for their own good? And due to this lack of *knowledge to produce*, they have their raw mineral resources sold to the so-called developed countries, and afterward, the same minerals resources are imported back to them as a finished product and at a higher price, and the money they were paid for the raw materials is taking back from them and even more. Does this explain why some countries are always borrowing money from the so-called developed countries, even when they have gold and diamonds beneath their soil? And by borrowing money, they become slaves to the lender and thereby fulfilling Proverbs 22:7?

The list of the oppression of the pride of men can go on and on *because the hearts of them that believe not have been blinded by the devil so that the light of God will not shine on them to save their souls.* (See 2 Corinthians 4:4).

My intent in this book is to share with you the knowledge of the wisdom of God that guarantees your exemption from any of the above oppressions, which is the mystery of the iniquity that is already at work in the world.

*"For **the mystery of iniquity doth already work**: only he who now letteth will let, until he be taken out of the way."* (2 Thessalonians 2:7). The lack of knowledge of the wisdom of God among men is the reason the world is perishing under the evil inventions of iniquity and lawlessness.

I pray that this book will not only bless your life with peace and prosperity but that you and your loved ones will always be exempted from the oppressions of the pride of man through the knowledge of the wisdom of divine security.

One

The Wisdom of Divine Peace

THE WISDOM OF DIVINE PEACE

In this first chapter of this book, I will be talking about the knowledge of the wisdom of divine peace, which is the Peace of God, so that you, the reader, perhaps, for the first time in your life, will understand what the Peace of God is and how to start walking in it for the rest of your life.

There is no peace in this world, or we can say the world has no peace to offer. That is why when a person transitions, many who sends their condolence messages to the deceased' family will say may his or her soul rest in peace. That means it's self-evident that there is no peace in this world, so the people presume that the person who transitioned did not have peace while he or she was alive here in this world.

You might have asked, or you may be asking now, as you are reading this book, if someone can still have peace in a world where one cannot turn on the TV or read the newspapers without hearing about a bomb going off in a city, or outbreaks of political crisis or virus, or about the world's economy heading for a crash, or a company going bankrupt and many becoming jobless? The answer to these questions is yes, you can still have peace in such a world, but you can't get that peace from this same world because this world has no peace to offer. You can only get peace from God, *the Peace of God that surpasses all understanding and reasoning.* (Philippians 4:7).

As I said in the introduction, you cannot stop or avert the oppression of the wicked in this world, but you can seek an exemption for yourself and your loved ones. If you read your Bible very well, you will see that there were famines, plagues, money failure, (economic crash), mass deaths, etc. But not everyone was affected. Those who were protected were those who connected to the covenant of exemption, and that covenant of exemption from all the oppressions of wickedness in this world is what this book is all about.

I will urge you, therefore, to be of an open heart to the teachings of this book, for the knowledge of the wisdom of God is for those whose heart is open to receive it. This is because the knowledge of the wisdom of God is so simple that many overlook it due to its simplicity. *"For God in his wisdom made it impossible for people to know him by means of their own wisdom. Instead, by means of the so-called foolish message we preach, God decided to save those who be-lieve"*. (1 Corinthians 1:21. GNT).

Believe in the so-called "foolish" message of preaching the gospel? Yes, that is the door that leads you to the knowledge of the wisdom of God for peace, prosperity, and security. With your heart now open, let us now begin our study by, first of all, understanding what the Peace of God is and how to start walking in it.

• *Understanding the Peace of God*

When we talk about the Peace of God that surpasses all understanding, you must understand what it is. Understanding the Peace of God brings home the knowledge of what to expect in your quest for divine peace. Therefore, in this section, you are going to, first of all, understand what the Peace of God is.

The Hebrew word for *peace* is called Šālôm, which means *peace in totality or completeness, success, fulfillment, wholeness, harmony, security, and well being.* Is there any country today where people can boast about this kind of definition of lifestyle? Of course not, even the United States, whose government claims to have the best of everything in the world, is today the most insecure place, and that is because the world has no peace to offer anyone, no matter the country of residence.

The Peace of God comes from God Himself. When you receive this peace, you start living a complete life of harmony and tranquillity, regardless of circumstances. You will no longer be afraid of the pride of man; instead, you will become a channel through which God will deliver those who are under the bondage of fear. The Peace of God is that inner tranquillity, that assurance, and trust, that inner conviction, where you just know that everything is fine, circumstances notwithstanding. The Peace of God is that state of rest, calmness, and serenity of spirit, that fearless countenance of a bold attitude with an absolute dependence on the power and wisdom of God.

The Peace of God can also be linked with faith, for you cannot claim to have faith in God if you don't have peace in your heart, for it's in that state of absolute peace that people can see and say that you have faith, for faith, the scripture says, *is to be sure of the things we hope for, to be certain of the things we cannot see.* (Hebrews 11:1).

You cannot claim to be *sure* of the things you hope for and be *certain* of the things you cannot see if you don't have peace in your heart. It's the Peace of God in your heart that empowers your acts of faith. The Peace of God in your heart is the evidence of your faith in the power and faithfulness of God to do what He has said in His Word.

The Peace of God is not the absence of fear or uncertainty; rather, it's the triumph over fear and uncertainty. In the midst of a windstorm, Jesus was at peace; (see Mark 4:37-39). Amid shipwreck and a venom, Paul was at peace; (see Acts 28:1-6). The Peace of God is your battle-ax; it's impossible to experience any defeat until you lose your peace, which is the evidence of your faith in the power and faithfulness of God.

I can't say I have not found myself in the middle of fear and uncertainty, but I can tell you that I have never lost the Peace of God in my heart in any of those undesirable circumstances because I know that as long as I hold my peace, I will always obtain victory.

As I write this book, I'm in Monclar De Quercy, France, with my wife and children, and we were supposed to travel to Lagos, Nigeria, in March. It was in this same month that the whole world locked down due to something they called covid-19. The stay at home order was issued, the social distancing was also required, and later the wearing of a face mask (which is medically unhealthy) was made obligatory. It was a challenging period, but there was nothing we could do but wait and pray for God to stop the enemy from carrying out his wicked plans, according to Psalm 33:10 and Psalm 140:8-13.

We had already packed all our bags and ready for departure on the 20th, only to get a call from the airline company on the 16th, saying that there has been a lockdown of airports in France and that they won't be able to fly until further notice. Businesses, workplaces, shops, places of worship, everything, and everyone was instructed by their governments to lockdown and stay at home with controlled and limited movements until further notice. The whole world was in total darkness (ignorant) of what was going on. Fear and uncertainty gripped humanity in every corner of the globe. Prices of foodstuffs increased rapidly due to limited supply.

The media houses all over the globe went out

of regular business and focused only on the false death rates across nations as if there was nothing else to talk about in the whole of planet earth. Yet, amid all the fear and the news of deaths rates from the media, my family and I never lost the Peace of God in our hearts; instead, we were praying for the restoration of the world and for miraculous healing on those hospitalized across nations due to fear, and also for divine judgment on those working with the enemy against humanity.

In that state of peace, I began to feel in my spirit that the whole thing about the so-called covid-19 might just be another oppression of the mystery of iniquity of this world. That is because my faith in God to heal and restore nations got more spirited as we prayed for the world. That is what the Peace of God does, it empowers you never to acknowledge the existence of fear, and since you cannot admit it fear, then to you, it does not exist; therefore, what affects others cannot affect you.

The Peace of God is that divine light that shines in your heart and fills your heart and mind with such joy and peace amid trouble that people will wonder what kind of a person are you. That was the response of the Disciples of Christ when He was at sleep amid windstorm, and then, after He arose and calmed the storm by His word, the disciples wondered, saying, *what manner of Man is this, that even the winds and the sea obey Him.* (Luke 8:25).

When you begin to walk in the Peace of God, people will start to wonder at you, because the Peace of God transcends and surpasses all understanding. The Peace of God guides you in making the right decisions; it's your umpire. It's through the Peace of God in your heart and mind that you walk in divine direction. In other words, it's through the Peace of God that you are divinely guided in all issues of life. (See Colossians 3:15).

I link peace with faith, because without peace in your heart, how can you say you have faith? For faith, the scripture says, *"is the assurance (title deed, confirmation) of things hoped for (divinely guaranteed), and the evidence of things not seen [the conviction of their reality, faith comprehends as fact what cannot be experienced by the physical senses].*" (Hebrews 11:1. AMP*).* That means the things you are hoping to see them manifest in the physical is something that you cannot experience or perceive by the senses, yet faith comprehends them as *fact.* Done!

How then can you, by faith, comprehend something as fact, and still be anxious? You see, this shows that the Peace of God in your heart and mind, then, is your proof that the matter is settled. This is what moves heaven to always respond in your favor. The scripture says; "*Do not be anxious or worried about anything, but in everything [every circumstance and situation] by prayer and petition with thanksgiving, continue to make your [specific] requests known to God. And the Peace of God [that peace which reassures the heart, that peace] which transcends all understanding, [that peace which] stands guard over your hearts and your minds in Christ Jesus [is yours].*" (Philippians 4:6-7. AMP).

Even in prayers, the Peace of God is your guide and guard. That means, after making your request known to God, you must check for the Peace of God for confirmation of the prayer. Now, if you are hoping to see the manifestation of the things you have requested from God in prayers, the Peace of God in your heart and mind, then, is what assures you that your prayers are answered. You are now empowered by that peace to act and speak in accordance with your hope; this then is called faith, because you have the Peace of God in your heart.

In Acts 16:25-34, Paul and Silas sang praises and prayed to God right inside the prison house, that is because they had the Peace of God in their hearts and minds. You cannot be singing praises and praying inside a prison house if you don't have the Peace of God in your heart, especially if you got arrested for what you believe, like in the case of Paul and Salas. But as they sang and prayed in the Peace of God, something supernatural took place. The prison foundation was shaken, the doors, bars, and the chains in Paul and Silas's hands were shattered into pieces, and everyone was set free, including the prison officer who received salvation. That is why the Scripture says that the Peace of God surpasses all understanding, that means nothing can comprehend the Peace of

God, and since nothing can comprehend it, then nothing can apprehend it, because the Peace of God comes from God Himself, and whatever God gives, He also protects.

The Peace of God is a supernatural force that operates in your heart and mind, regardless of whatever that may be going on around you. The Peace of God, operating in your heart, makes everything to work in your favor. In 1 Kings 4:25, the Scripture says that *there was peace in all Israel and Judah* during the forty years reign of King Solomon, and in 1 Kings 5:4, Solomon himself said; *"But now the LORD my God hath given me rest on every side, so that there is neither adversary nor evil occurrent."* That was because Solomon was a man who governed Israel through the knowledge of the wisdom of God, and by that wisdom, he enjoyed supernatural peace that brought about the rest in all Israel and Judah. Solomon led Israel as a King for forty years, and there was no war, no famine, and no plague of any kind, no money failure, or any such thing. That was because King Solomon led Israel and Judah by the knowledge of the wisdom of God and operated on the frequency of divine peace, prosperity, and security that automatically made Israel and Judah experienced such peace, prosperity, and security for the forty years of King Solomon's leadership.

Lack of knowledge of the wisdom of God among leaders today is the reason why the whole world is suffering from one disaster to another, and everyone seems to be following the so-called democracy without any demand for transparency. Is there any leader of any nation on this earth today who will say he or she is leading by the knowledge of the wisdom of God? No, they developed their own wisdom, which has done more harm to humanity than good, which is why the Scripture says that *"even what seems to be God's foolishness is wiser than human wisdom, and what seems to be God's weakness is stronger than human strength."* (1 Corinthians 1:25. GNT).

The Peace of God in your heart is what resists and defeats the enemy. As they faced the red sea, gripped by fear as the enemy and his armies were coming after them from behind, Moses, the man of God, full of the Peace of God, said to the people:

"The Lord will fight for you while you [only need to] keep silent and remain calm." (Exodus 14:14. AMP). To be calm means to be at peace, and here Moses was telling them to remain calm, which means don't lose your peace, don't agitate, and don't be afraid even if you have every reason to.

Again the Peace of God is your guide and guard; it protects you from evil and from the pride of man. The weapon of the enemy is fear, and the purpose of fear is to make you lose your peace, and until you lose your peace, evil cannot touch you. The Peace of God, therefore, is your shield of faith, with which you quench and annul all the fiery arrows of the wicked. (See Ephesians 6:15-16). The Peace of God is that inner tranquillity of the spirit that fills you up with joy, calmness and makes you fearless even amid fear. The world cannot give such peace because the world doesn't have it. You can only give what you have, and the only thing the world has to give is fear, and this is because fear is the enemy's power through which he controls human beings. Meaning that you cannot be controlled if you are fearless and full of the Peace of God in your heart and mind.

I read a story about a certain man of God who was on a flight for a journey, and soon after departure, the captain announced that they will have to battle through bad weather for some minutes and that everyone should be on their seatbelts. Shortly after the announcement, the airplane began to shake and vibrate, and everyone on board was alarmed, and then the man of God noticed that someone just left his seat and came and sat in the vacant seat next to him. The shaking in the flight continued for about fifteen more minutes, and then everything returned to normal, and there was calm and stability.

When they finally landed in their destination, the man approached the man of God and began to explain to him the reason why he left his seat to sit next to him. He said he saw how calm and peaceful the man of God was amid that vibration in the flight, and that knowing him as a pastor, he came and sat next to him so that if eventually, the flight was to crash, he will grab him, and two of them will disappear together and reappear somewhere safe after the crash, that he believed that God would send an angel to supernaturally take the man of God out of the flight to somewhere safe if the airplane was to crash. The man of God was touched by the man's faith about God sending an angel to save him if the airplane was to crash, so he invited him to their church for the following Sunday service, and he came, and during the altar call, he was among the people that came out and he received salvation on the spot.

Now, what convinced that man to believe that the man of God can be supernaturally protected if the flight was to crash? It was the Peace of God. He could see that inner tranquillity of the spirit, soul, and body in the man of God. He could see that the man of God was not troubled in any way at all, even when everyone on board was agitating, yet the man of God was as calm and peaceful as a baby asleep in his or her mother's arms. That peace and inner tranquillity of the spirit is the evidence of that man of God's faith in the power and faithfulness of God to protect him in times of trouble and uncertainty. (See Jeremiah 17: 8). The Peace of God must be evident in your life. People must be able to see that tranquillity of the spirit in you.

That is what convinces them that you have faith in God, and by this evidence of faith through peace, you can win many to Christ. Faith in God must be seen through the Peace of God in your heart and mind reflecting in your countenance.

There are millions, even billions of people around the world who do not have peace, and that is because the world has no peace to offer. The reason why the technology and fashion industries are booming is that people are trying to get peace by going after new inventions of technology. They buy the new model of cars, phones, TV sets, and furniture. New houses, the latest fashion in town, they fly business class for holiday tours and sleep in luxury hotels. All this is because they want to have peace and be happy. But what they don't know is that, in as much as these things are excellent and necessary for life, yet they don't give one peace because the Peace of God that surpasses all understanding does not come from acquiring the luxury things of this world but in iand from God.

The reason why the rate of divorce keeps going higher around the world, especially in the west, is that they think that the new husband or wife will make them have peace. There are lots of super-rich people who are unhappy and without peace. Most of them have gone through divorce many times, yet no peace at all. That is because, in their knowledge of acquiring riches, they lack the knowledge of the wisdom of God for divine peace, and that is because the principalities and powers of this world have blinded the minds of many, so that the light of God, through the gospel of Christ, will not shine on them and give them salvation and peace. (See Ephesians 6:12) and (2 Corinthians 4:4). The Peace of God cannot be bought with money or with the luxuries of this world. In as much as it's good to enjoy the luxury things of this world, if one can afford them in the right way, one must not put his or her trust in them for peace. The Bible says *"he that trusts in his riches will fall."* (Proverbs 11:28). And in Psalm 62:10, the Scripture declares that *"if riches increase, set not your heart (do not trust) in them."* That means riches can increase, as long as you are still engaged in servicing the needs of humanity in one way or another, but you are not to set your heart in the riches but in God, who gives us all things richly to enjoy. (See 1 Timothy 6:17).

As a little boy growing up in a humble family of eight, and having left my parents at the age of eight to live with an aunt, who raised me with solid Christian principles, which I believe has contributed significantly to my Christian walk today. At that early stage of my life, I was obliged to always fast every Sunday together with everyone in the house. The fasting ends after we return from the church at 2: pm. Every morning I would be the one to read aloud the Scriptures for the morning prayers, and sometimes I have to also say the morning prayers after reading aloud the Scriptures. I was also taught about the principles of giving and tithing, by taking out of my school pocket money, ten percent of it, which I receive every school day as I get ready for school. This money is then brought before my aunt for inspection every Sunday morning as we all get ready for church. She will tell me to take it with me to the church, and during offering time, I will drop it in the offering basket.

As a little child then, I always dream of having the best things in this world so that I can have peace. I used to think back then, as a little child with dreams and aspirations in my heart, that one cannot have peace if one lacks all the beautiful and luxurious things of this world. But never did I know that riches are for service and pleasure, and never gives one peace. Today as a husband, father, author, and pastor, and having learned from the school of life through the wisdom of God, I have come to understand that peace, *that peace that surpasses all understanding,* comes only from God and not from riches. *"Thou wilt keep him in perfect peace, whose mind is stayed on thee: because he trusteth in thee."* (Isaiah 26:3). You enjoy perfect peace when you put your trust in God. The Peace of God in your heart, which is your evidence of faith in God, is what causes you always to obtain victory. It also means that with the Peace of God in your heart, nothing can make you fall or stumble. You will always live above the worries of this world. (See Psalm 119:165).

The Peace of God always triggers the miraculous in your favor. In 1 Samuel 1:7-28, we read about the story of Hannah, who was childless, and as a result of her childlessness she was always sad, meaning that she had no peace of mind. Sometimes she will cry and refuse to eat because her co-wife repeatedly mocks her and reminded her of her barrenness. But the Bible says in verse 9, that as they were in Shiloh, Hannah suddenly *rose up* and engaged God in prayer, and it was in that effectual and fervent prayer that she obtained the Peace of God that surpasses all understanding, and that peace of God in her heart triggered the miraculous in her life and she conceived and gave us the great prophet, Samuel. She became so peaceful after the prayer that the Scripture says that *the woman went her way, and did eat, and her countenance was no more sad.* (See 1 Samuel 1:18). That is the triumphant power of the Peace of God in your heart. It makes you be at rest in the midst of turmoil and turns everything around in your favor.

However, you must also understand that happiness cannot be mistaken or substituted for the Peace of God that surpasses all understanding. Happiness is a feeling. It's a state of mind, which can be triggered by the acquisition of material things or the experiences of some nature. You can choose to be happy, and you can also choose not to be happy. It all depends on what activities you engage in as time passes. It means that happiness is of one's making. Engaging in activities like exercising, reading, spending time with family and friends can make one less sensitive to negative emotions and trigger the state or feelings of happiness. Hanging out and chatting with friends and families is also a great way to stir up feelings of happiness.

People have different kinds of activities that make them happy; for some, it's their jobs, and people who love what they do succeed significantly in life. For some, it's spending quality and intimate time with their spouse, which is very healthy for married couples. There are also people whose happiness is derived from helping out with some charity activities like taking care of children at the orphanage homes and so forth. Some of the activities that make me happy are reading, exercising, and speaking to the audience on biblical applications for successful and prosperous living and the achievement of goals. The author also enjoys spending quality time with his family, traveling, and shopping of books not excluded. In as much as we all have some positive and creative activities that make us happy in our lives, yet, it cannot and should not be mistaken or substituted for the Peace of God.

Now, having understood the Peace of God and what it does for and in one's life, let me now proceed to unveil to you, the reader, the gateway to God's Peace, so that you can begin to operate and function in *the Peace of God that surpasses all understanding.*

• *Walking In the Peace of God*

Acquaint now thyself with him, and be at peace: thereby good shall come unto thee. Receive, I pray thee, the law from his mouth, and lay up his words in thine heart. (Job 22:21-22).

To walk in the Peace of God, that peace that surpasses all understanding, *you must have Peace with God.* You cannot have the Peace of God if you are not at peace with God. Peace with God is what automatically releases the Peace of God into your heart and mind, and you begin to live above the adverse circumstances of this world.

As we proceed in this section of walking in the Peace of God, it's crucial that you understand, first of all, that you are a spiritual being with a soul, and you are living in a body inhabiting a physical world. You were made in the image and likeness of God with all power and authority to dominate the earth and subdue it. (See Genesis 1:26-27). This *dominion mandate* is not without the Peace of God, which means that the Peace of God that surpasses all understanding was part of your making, for God, your Maker, is the God of Peace. (See 1 Thessalonians 5:23). You were fashioned to operate and function in the Peace of God, the phenomenal consciousness of His presence in you and around you, and the consciousness of *the effectual workings of His mighty power in your favor any day, anytime, and anywhere.* The Peace of God, this tranquillity of the spirit, is the crown of your divine mandate to dominate and subdue the earth for His glory. Peace with God, therefore, is the requirement to walking in the Peace of God.

Humanity is suffering from the consequences of spiritual death. Only salvation can resurrect anyone from this spiritual death caused by Adam's disobedience and rebellion towards God. The treason committed by Adam caused the whole of the human race to die spiritually to God. As a result of this tragedy, the Peace of God that man once enjoyed departed, and the entire human race was subjected to fear, which is the power of the enemy to control and rule over lives. Fear is a product of ignorance, which is the lack of knowledge of God. Ignorance, therefore, is your worst enemy, and you must fight it with everything at your disposal.

The disobedience and rebellion of Adam towards God is the highest treason ever committed in the history of creation, and the consequence or upshot is spiritual death, which means to be separated from God. For ages, man lived in that state of separation from his Maker and knowing deep down in his soul that something is missing, man created all kinds of false religions, idol worship, sects, unrighteous and wicked practices of all kinds in search of God, or that *spiritual self* that is missing. At a time, some began to conclude and say in their hearts that there is no God because all their attempts to find God through false religions failed. These are the people the Bible calls fools because they believe in their hearts that there is no God. (See Psalm 14:1).

In Romans 5:14 the Scripture says; "*Nevertheless, death reigned from Adam to Moses, even over them that had not sinned after the similitude of Adam's transgression, who is the figure of him that was to come.*" From Adam to Moses, humanity lived in this state of spiritual death, which is the complete separation from God. Notice it didn't say death reigned from Adam to Christ. That is because Christ is the fulfillment of the gospel of salvation that God first preached to Adam and Eve when He clothed them with animal skin shortly after the treason was committed. By clothing Adam and Eve with animal skin, God foretold the redemptive work of Christ that will clothe humanity with salvation. (See Genesis 3:21) and also (Isaiah 61:10).

Before this time, God spoke only through se-lected few, which we call holy prophets. All of them saw and prophesied about the coming of Christ, who will pay the ultimate price with His blood for the treason committed by Adam. By His blood, He will obtain eternal redemption for hu-manity, which means that the door to God will once again be opened, and anyone who will believe and identify with the redemptive work of Christ will be recreated and made to have Peace with God through Him. *"For as by one man's disobedience many were made sinners, so by the obedience of one shall many be made righteous."* (Romans 5:19).

That is the gospel, and it's what we are preach-ing to the world. It means that the same way all human beings became victims of spiritual death by Adam's disobedience, in that same way, many will be made righteous by the obedience of Christ. Today, salvation has been offered to humanity through the redemptive work of Christ, and anyone who believes in the death and resurrection of Christ will be Born-Again (Recreated) with everlasting life and peace with God. The Scripture says: "for the wages of sin is death; but the gift of God is eternal life through Jesus Christ our Lord." (Romans 6:23). The wages of Adam's disobedience is spiritual death, and this death came upon all human beings. Therefore for salvation to be possible, Christ has to die, meaning that He must identify with man's death, and then by the resurrection from the dead comes the new life, and this new life is everlasting. It's without any history of sin. *"For he hath made him to be sin for us, who knew no sin; that we might be made the righteousness of God in him."* (2 Corinthians 5:21).

In the redemptive plan of God, the person who must die for humanity must be someone who never knew sin. Someone as Holy and Righteous as God Himself. That is the only sacrifice that will be acceptable for salvation to be made possible for the human race. Since no one is holy and righteous in the whole universe, God himself has to come in the form of Man, which is Christ, and by the death and resurrection of Christ, salvation is made possible to all who will believe. On the day of the crucifixion of Christ, heaven was silent. That was because it's the demand of justice for the redemption of humanity. From the time of Christ's arrest to the time He died and was buried, no angel dared to step an inch into the scene. The whole of heaven was in a standstill. Even in Matthew 26:39-45, He prayed to the father, but there was no answer from heaven. It was only on the point of resurrection that heaven dispatched angels because now salvation has come, *it's done, it's finished,* and now we have the victory. That is because, to set man free from spiritual death, the Holy One must taste death, go to hell, defeat him that has the power of death in hell, and resurrect back to live triumphantly. (See Colossians 2:14-15). That is the only legal ground by which salvation can come to humanity. That is the victory we have in Christ today, and that is the mystery of salvation.

Therefore, to be Born-Again, you must identify yourself with the death and resurrection of Christ, because He died for you. By acknowledging and identifying yourself with His death, you accept that you died when He died because *the wages of sin is death*. Also, by acknowledging and identifying yourself with His resurrection, you accept that you have resurrected from spiritual death because when He resurrected, you also resurrected with Him, and you are seated with Him in the heavenly place far above all principalities and powers. "*And hath raised us up together, and made us sit together in heavenly places in Christ Jesus*". (Ephesians 2:6). That is what it means to be Born-Again (Recreated). It's believing with all your heart that He died and confessing with your mouth that He resurrected for your justification, making you pure and righteous before God in Him. The Scripture declares: "Therefore being justified by faith, we have peace with God through our Lord Jesus Christ." (Romans 5:1).

It's important to note here that anyone who is not in Christ, anyone who has not acknowledged and identified with the death and resurrection of Christ is still under the wages of Adam's disobedience, which is spiritual death. Look, this is not about being civilized or having worldly knowledge acquired from all the prominent universities of this world and thinking that you are wise. *"Woe is unto them that are wise in their own eyes, and prudent in their own sight!"* (Isaiah 5:21). And *"Seest thou a man wise in his own conceit? there is more hope of a fool than of him".* (Proverbs 26:12). This is not about Harvard, Oxford, or Yale. Anyone who has not been recreated in Christ is spiritually dead, no matter the person's social status or wealth. This is why the Scripture says in Proverbs 21:16 that *"The man that wandereth out of the way of understanding (godly Wisdom) shall remain in the congregation of the dead."* Is that really in the Bible? You may ask, oh yes it is, and that's what you just read. The *Godly Wisdom* here refers to the wisdom of God for salvation, which is what I'm sharing with you in this book.

To walk in the Peace of God, you must trust absolutely on God. You cannot put your trust in the wisdom of men and expect to have the Peace of God in your heart and mind. The Scripture declares: "*Neither is there salvation in any other: for there is none other name under heaven given among men, whereby we must be saved.*" (Acts 4:12). Did you see that? It's very clear. Salvation can only be found in Christ, not in anywhere or anything else. This is why the enemy is using every means, on a daily basis, to ensure many don't accept Christ and have peace with God because the devil knows that without accepting Christ as Lord, there is no way anyone can receive salvation and be free from the wages of Adam's disobedience, which is spiritual death. "*For he who has the Son has life; he who does not have the Son of God does not have life*". (1 John 5:12).

The fact that the redemptive work of Christ has been accomplished does not mean that the whole of the human race is free from spiritual death. That is what a lot of people think, but that is wrong, it's not true. Yes, the redemptive work of Christ has been accomplished, but it must be practically acknowledged, believed, and confessed by each person before salvation, and Peace with God can be credited on that person's account. Read the following verse carefully to understand this better:

"*But what does it say? "The word is near you, in your mouth and in your heart" that is, the word [the message, the basis] of faith which we preach, because if you acknowledge and confess with your mouth that Jesus is Lord [recognizing His power, authority, and majesty as God], and believe in your heart that God raised Him from the dead, you will be saved. For* **with the heart** *a person believes [in Christ as Savior] resulting in his justification [that is, being made righteous, being freed of the guilt of sin and made acceptable to God]; and* **with the mouth** *he acknowledges and confesses [his faith openly], resulting in and confirming [his] salvation*". (Romans 10:8-10. AMP).

That is the Biblical way of receiving salvation. You must practically come to Christ and then acknowledge and identify with His death and resurrection, which is also your death and resurrection into everlasting life and peace with God. To have peace with God through Christ, you must confess with your mouth and believe with your heart. That is how it works because you cannot believe and not confess what you believe. "*The scripture says, "I spoke because I believed. In the same spirit of faith, we also speak because we believe*". (2 Corinthians 4:13.

GNT). The problem with a lot of Christians all over the world is that they are not speaking what the Scripture says, the word of faith which they say they believe. (See Romans 10:8). Instead, they are communicating with what they see and hear in the media, which is the enemy's voice of fear, and remember, fear is the enemy's power to control and rule over lives. It's his weapon of mass destruction. Until you are afraid, the enemy is powerless before you. This is why you must immerse yourself in the study of Scriptures daily because it fuels your faith. Knowledge of the Scriptures is what makes you wise unto salvation and empowers you to possess your possession. (See 2 Timothy 3:15).

When you are bankrupt of Scriptures, then you cannot speak faith. That is why many speak fear because they are bankrupt of Scriptures, which is the word of faith. That explains why the enemy is blinding minds about the Scriptures; so that he can continue to rule over them in darkness (ignorance) (See 2 Corinthians 4:4). Salvation and the practical knowledge of the wisdom of God are the winning secrets of life. (See Ephesians 6:17). Now let's get down to the main thing here, which is the Biblical way of receiving salvation. We have explained in detail that you must acknowledge and identify yourself with the death and resurrection of Christ, but in receiving salvation, you don't confess the death, because the death of Christ is the enemy's defeat. *"None of the rulers of this world knew this wisdom. If they had known it, they would not have crucified the Lord of Glory"*. (1 Corinthians 2:8. GNT). But the resurrection of Christ is where you come in. It's your justification to have everlasting life and peace with God through Christ.

So, in receiving salvation, you must open your mouth and confess aloud, the Lordship of Christ in a change of mind (repentance) and call on Him to come and live in your heart by His Holy Spirit. Then you must believe with your heart that *He resurrected from the dead for your justification* into everlasting life, then you confess, affirm and proclaim, that you are now saved.

So if you are not yet Born-Again and you are reading this book, then I'm glad to lead you through the Biblical way of receiving salvation so that you can start living a new life in Christ with the Peace of God that surpasses all understanding.

Now, put this book in a readable position, raise your right hand up, and then read aloud the below prayer of salvation. Let the whole of your being surrender to Him as you read this prayer. This is your opportunity to be in Christ, so don't joke with it. I will be waiting for you in the next paragraph to congratulate and welcome you into the kingdom of Christ.

Prayer of Salvation

Dear Lord Jesus, I thank You for this opportunity to come to you today. I confess right now with my mouth that You are Lord of my life, and I believe in my heart that You resurrected from the dead for my justification. Now I'm justified; I'm free, and I'm saved. Thank You, Lord Jesus, for saving me, Amen.

Congratulations! You have just been translated from darkness to light and from death to everlasting life. You are now at peace with God through Christ. From this minute, you are no more under the wages of sin, which is death, you are now a new creature in Christ, and this new creature (*you*) has no history of sin. (See 2 Corinthians 5:17). The life you just received now is a brand new life in Christ, which is the very life of God; (Zoe) because *your life is now hidden with Christ in God.* (See Colossians 3:3). You are now a uniquely recreated and superior being with all power and authority to have dominion on earth. *"Likewise, reckon ye also yourselves to be dead indeed unto sin, but alive unto God through Jesus Christ our Lord."* (Romans 6:11).

You are now dead unto sin, which means you are no more under the wages of Adam's disobedience, and the power of sin cannot have dominion over you anymore. You are now alive unto God through Christ. Heaven is celebrating you right now because there is more joy (celebration) in heaven over one soul that is saved. (See Luke 15:7). You are now a citizen and an ambassador of the kingdom of Christ. Angels are now assigned to minister to your needs here on earth. Whatever you need, just telephone heaven in prayer, and it will be done. (See Hebrews 1:14). From this minute, you will never be stranded anymore. Christ is now living in your heart by His Holy Spirit. Anytime the enemy launches his attacks, the Spirit of the Lord will lift up a standard against him in your favor. (See Isaiah 59:19).

But wait, what about *the Peace of God that surpasses all understanding*? Sure, it has been credited to your account the moment you made that confession of faith. The Peace of God is now released into your heart, and I'm sure you are already feeling it in your spirit. Look at the words of Christ to you; *"Peace I leave with you; My [perfect] Peace I give to you; not as the world gives do I give to you. Do not let your heart be troubled, nor let it be afraid. [Let My perfect peace calm you in every circumstance and give you courage and strength for every challenge]"*. (John 14: 27. AMP). That is it. He has given you His Peace, which is *the Peace of God that surpasses all understanding*. You cannot confess Christ as Lord and not receive His Peace, because, as you have already studied in this chapter so far, the Peace of God is what makes you calm in every circumstance and gives you courage and strength for every challenge, and that is what you just read in the above verse. That is the Peace you have just received as a new creature in Christ Jesus.

By having Peace with God through Christ, you are now walking in the Peace of God that surpasses all understanding. Peace with God is the eternal covenant that exempts you from the operations of the enemy. As the enemy launches out his attacks on humanity from time to time, you shall be exempted. *"For when thou passest through the waters, I will be with thee; and through the rivers, they shall not overflow thee: when thou walkest through the fire, thou shalt not be burned; neither shall the flame kindle upon thee."* (Isaiah 43:2). Did you notice it says **When** thou passest through the waters, not **if** thou passest through the waters? It means that until Jesus returns, there will always be a global economic crash, political crisis, wars, outbreaks of viruses, killings, bombings, earthquakes, hurricanes, tsunamis, windstorms, etc. You cannot stop any of these attacks from the enemy against humanity, but you and your loved ones will be exempted for His glory.

As I closed this chapter, I want you to understand that the strength of salvation is the practical knowledge of the Scriptures. *"wisdom and knowledge shall be the stability of thy times, and **strength of salvation**: the fear of the LORD is his treasure."* (Isaiah 33:6). So you must immerse yourself deeply into the ocean of divine revelation through an intense and radical study of the Scriptures. Like the great man of God, Bishop David O. Oyedepo, said: *"The study of scriptures is not a transferable responsibility."* So you must study for yourself to gain practical knowledge of the Scriptures and apply them to your life as well. Knowledge is not power until it's applied for the greater good. The same way you cannot tell anybody to eat for you when you are famished, that same way nobody can study the Scriptures for you.

The Scripture says: *"So then, my dear ones, just as you have always obeyed [my instructions with enthusiasm], not only in my presence, but now much more in my absence, **continue** to work out your salvation [that is, cultivate it, bring it to full effect, actively pursue **spiritual maturity**] with awe-inspired fear and trembling [using serious caution and critical self-evaluation* *to avoid anything that might offend God or discredit the name of Christ*]." (Philippians 2:12. AMP).

In working out your salvation, you will need your own light from the Scriptures to determine your own speed in the race of life. Divine revelation gained through intense study of Scriptures boosts your faith, peace, and everything else you have received in salvation. (See Acts 20:32).

Two

The Wisdom of Divine Prosperity

THE WISDOM OF DIVINE PROSPERITY

The knowledge of the wisdom of divine prosperity is for the spiritual and not for the carnal. It's for those who walk by the instructions of the Spirit, and not by the sensory perceptions of the flesh. It's for those who understand divine prosperity and its terms and then position themselves on that platform. *"For strong meat belongeth to them that are of full age, even those who by reason of use have their senses exercised to discern both good and evil."* (Hebrews 5:14). The knowledge of the wisdom of divine prosperity is strong meat, and strong meat is not for children; it's for those who are of full age (spiritually mature) who by reason of use, have had their spiritual senses exercised to discern (distinguish) between good and evil. You cannot be carnal minded and expect to possess the knowledge of the wisdom of divine prosperity. *"For the natural man receiveth not the things of the Spirit of God: for they are foolishness unto him: neither can he know them, because they are spiritually discerned."* (1 Corinthians 2:14).

The reason why many Christians are struggling with poverty all over the world is that they are still babes sucking milk when they should have graduated into eating not only meat but meat with bone. In working out your salvation to the level of enjoying not only divine peace but also divine prosperity, you must be a hardcore spiritual person, which is living according to the revelations of Scriptures as revealed to you by the Spirit from time to time. Jesus made it clear when He said; *"whosoever heareth these sayings of mine and doeth them, I will liken him unto a wise man, which built his house upon a rock: And the rain descended, and the floods came, and the winds blew, and beat upon that house; **and it fell not: for it was founded upon a rock**. And every one that heareth these sayings of mine, and doeth them not, shall be likened unto a foolish man, which built his house upon the sand: And the rain descended, and the floods came, and the winds blew, and beat upon that house; and it fell: and great was the fall of it"*. (Matthew 7:24-27).

Spirituality must be your lifestyle to experience divine prosperity. You must be living and conducting your life according to the teachings of the gospel of Christ. That is what it means to be spiritual as a Christian. Also, the knowledge of the wisdom of divine prosperity is for those who have made themselves available to be used by God for His kingdom and for servicing the needs of humanity. Wealth in the kingdom of God is a function of selfless service for the kingdom of God and to human needs. When God was declaring His blessings on Abraham, He made the basis clear when He said: *"And I will make of thee a great nation, and I will bless thee, and make thy name great; **and thou shalt be a blessing.**"* (Genesis 12:2). The basis of God's blessings on him was that Abraham must be a *blessing*. Anyone who wants to acquire wealth for his or her own personal consumption is a fool. (See Luke 12:16-21).

The purpose of wealth is to bless nations through service. No one is permitted to acquire wealth if he or she has no heart to bless humanity through service in one way or another. Therefore, service, which is adding value to humanity through the kingdom, is where the dignity of life is bestowed. *"But Jesus called them to Himself and said,*

"You know that the rulers of the Gentiles have absolute power and lord it over them, and their great men exercise authority over them [tyrannizing them]. It is not this way among you, but whoever wishes to become great among you shall be your servant...". (Matthew 20:25-26. AMP)

When I talk about divine prosperity, I'm not talking about the prosperity of the world that is here today, and tomorrow you can't find it anymore. The world is very good at offering vanity in abundance. Get rich today, and tomorrow everything is gone. That is the way of the world, and that is why there were lots of rich people yesterday whose riches are nowhere to be found today because wealth gotten by vanity shall be diminished. (See Proverbs 13:11).

Anything that is not adding value to humanity in any way or solving human problems in one way or another is something that will soon crash and disappear into thin air as if it never existed. Wealth does not fall from heaven into your hands. It's by labor that you gather and accumulate wealth. For *"he that gathereth by labour shall in-*

crease." (Proverbs 13:11). When you labor for God's kingdom and in servicing the needs of humanity in one way or another, then your wealth will know no bounds.

Prosperity in God's perspective is not limited to financial success, but that is what comes to the minds of the majority of people when they hear the Word prosperity. Prosperity is the will of God for you because it involves everything about your life, both spiritually and physically. "*Beloved, I wish above all things that thou mayest prosper and be in health, even as thy soul prospereth*". (3 John: 2). Vibrant health, sound mind, joyful marriage, financial success or call it *too much money*, obedient and intelligent children, good and loving wife or husband, long life, fruitfulness, the list can go on, all these are inside the package of divine prosperity, and it's God's will for you to have and enjoy all these things in overabundance as long as you are in service and in obedient to His will. (See Job 36:11).

You may be asking now if it's possible to have and enjoy divine prosperity as defined above. The answer is one hundred percent yes. You can have and enjoy divine prosperity and even more, because as a child of God in Christ, *nothing is too big for you*, except that which is too big for your mind to comprehend and apprehend. Abraham, as mentioned above, is the symbol of divine prosperity in Scriptures, and in Genesis 24:1, the Bible says that *"Abraham was old, and well stricken in age: **and the Lord had blessed Abraham in all things.**"* To be blessed by God in all things is what we call *divine prosperity*. Remember also, that father Abraham was called the friend of God; (see James 2:23). Which means that Abraham was a hardcore spiritual man who walked with God and *believed God in all things, and God blessed him in all things.* (See Romans 4:3).

In this chapter, I will be taking you through the journey of understanding what divine prosperity is and how you can begin to walk in it.

• *Understanding Divine Prosperity*

Anything good and perfect comes from God and not from the world. (See James 1:17). The world has nothing good and perfect to offer anyone. Anything the world is offering you is either at the expense of your health, your marriage, your children, your peace of mind, or even your life. Anything that costs you any of these things is not good, and it's not perfect; it's from the world and from such, turn away.

As a child of God in Christ, you are in the world but not of the world. You don't believe what the world believes; you don't think and see things the way the world does. You don't process thoughts the same way the world process thoughts. You are the light of the world (See Matthew 5:14), meaning that you are to show the world the way to go and not the other way round. You are to rule and have dominion over all the earth (See Genesis 1:26) and not the world controlling and having authority over you.

Divine prosperity is one of your inheritances

in salvation. It's the prosperity of the spirit, soul, and body. It covers every aspect of your life and beyond. (3 John: 2). Divine prosperity is that state of abundance of every good thing that pertains to life and godliness. It's a life you live in peace and joy without any lack or breakdowns on your health or anything. It's a super-abundant life that flows from you to one generation after another in your family line.

We understand from Scriptures that *"The blessing of the Lord brings [true] riches, And He adds no sorrow to it [for it comes as a blessing from God]."* (Proverbs 10:22. AMP). In this world, you can be rich without been blessed, but you cannot be blessed without been *truly rich* because the blessing of the Lord makes you truly rich, and it adds no sorrow of any kind to it.

When God blesses you on the basis of you becoming a channel through which He blesses others, nothing can stop or hinder that blessing upon your life. Because of the blessing, God will curse anyone who attempts to curse you, and He will bless anyone who blesses you. He will be an enemy to your enemies and an adversary to your adversaries, all because you are a carrier of His blessing on the earth. (See Genesis 12:3, and also Exodus 23:22).

The blessing of the Lord in anyone's life is not for that individual alone. When God blesses you, it's because He wants to use you to bless your family, your community, your country, or the world at large. When you refuse to be a blessing, you limit the flow of the blessing in your own personal life. The blessing of the Lord is irreversible. When God blesses you, the blessing outlives you to generations after you, and this is as long as the channel to being a blessing to God's kingdom and to humanity remains open in your family line. This is why you will find around the world today, families whose businesses and wealth continue to serve humanity generations after generations. Examples are Kongo Gumi, a Japanese' family-run business of 1,400 years old, also known as the world's oldest family company, which is still in operation as I write this book. That is because the spiritual principles upon which the company was founded in 578 AD by its founder Shigemitsu Kongō, is still maintained by the family to date. Nishiyama Onsen Keiunkan, a hot spring hotel in Hayakawa, Japan, also known as the second oldest company in the world, has been managed for over 1,300 years by the same family of the founder, and it's still in operation as I write this book. Otterton Mill of United Kingdom, Château de Goulaine of France, and Staffelter Hof of Germany, to mention a few, all these family businesses are still in operation to date.

The significant thing about all these family-owned businesses around the world is that they have outlasted governments, nations, and cities. With all the wars, global economic crash, and plagues that have hit the world, you still find these companies doing business as usual. What then can be said to be the secret behind the longevity of these wealthy families and their businesses around the world? Is there some kind of managerial skill they posses or something? Of cause not, *it's the blessing of the Lord.* If you check very well, you will see that these companies are doing the same kind of businesses or services that other companies that have died out were also doing. So, you can see that it's the blessing of the Lord in what you are doing that makes the difference in your life and distinguishes you from others.

Don't let the devil deceive you into trusting in your own wisdom acquired through sense knowledge of this world. *"For the wisdom of this world is foolishness with God."* (See 1 Corinthians 3:19). The blessing of the Lord is what makes you rich, and it sustains and turns that riches into trans-generational wealth. *"But thou shalt remember the Lord thy God: for it is he that giveth thee power to get wealth, that he may establish his covenant which he sware unto thy fathers, as it is this day."* (Deuteronomy 8:18). It's God who gives the power (ability) to get wealth so that He can continue to establish His covenant on the earth as He swore to Abraham, and the covenant God had with Abraham was that He will bless him and he (Abraham) will be a blessing. So the ultimate purpose of God's blessing on our lives is first for His kingdom and to the service of humanity.

Divine prosperity is when the blessing of the Lord is upon the works of your hands. We saw this divine prosperity in the life of David, whom God blessed as a shepherd boy, and from the time that the blessing came upon him, he prospered in everything he did and in every way. (See 1 Samuel 18:14). He killed the giant Goliath, prevailed against the envy of king Saul, survived the coup d'état in his own palace, fought many wars, and yet he never lost in any of the battles, rather he won in all the battles he fought and reigned as king of Israel for forty years. David acquired great wealth, and he died at a very old age, and his son Solomon reigned even greater in Israel. That is the blessing of the Lord. It makes you wealthy; it preserves you and keeps you safe from every envy and pride of men.

When God blesses you, He qualifies you for the blessing, and this qualification is not on the world standard but on God's standard. When the blessing of the Lord is upon your life, you will prosper in everything you do, because it's God who justifies you and makes you right to Himself in Christ. *"For the Lord said unto Samuel, Look not on his countenance, or on the height of his stature; because I have refused him: for the Lord seeth not as man seeth; for* *man looketh on the outward appearance, **but the Lord looketh on the heart.*** " (1 Samuel 16:7).

When I got my call into the ministry, some friends of mine couldn't understand it, and that is because people always seem to judge you based on the world standard. After all, the world looks at your physical appearance or qualification, but God looks at your heart. Today I have written books that are bestsellers, and our young ministry and bookstores are growing and expanding with speed. Lives are being impacted and transformed for greater glory by the power of God's Word. That is the blessing of the Lord, and we are just beginning.

The life of Michael Faraday is an inspiring one, which I would love to reference here. If you are a student of electromagnetism and electrochemistry, then you must have come across the name Michael Faraday. He is one of the greatest scientists in history. His main discoveries include the principles underlying electromagnetic induction, diamagnetism, and electrolysis. He was a devout member and elder of the Sandemanian church. He was a man who self-educated himself into becoming a great scientist, and he excelled in chemistry and physics and became one of the most influential thinkers in history. But a careful study of the life of this great man reveals that Mr. Faraday was a man who remained absolutely committed to Biblical truth from his early childhood and throughout his long life.

Think about the things that run on electric motors like automobiles, fans, clocks, airplanes, pumps, vacuum cleaners, and so much more, and you will begin to get a hint of what Michael Faraday's work brought forth to humanity. It was said that the wealth generated by the inventions based on Michael Faraday's discoveries exceeded the value of the British stock exchange at the time. When the queen wanted to knight him, he declined, wishing to remain just Mr. Faraday to the end. It was said that the glory of Jesus Christ was the only reward he sought. Further studies showed that nothing mattered to him as much as one thing: his faith in Christ, and that he would instead prefer to be praying and studying the Bible with his fellow church members than be at an awards ceremony or have an audience with royalty.

Studies on the life of this great man further reveal that he saw himself as just a man whom God has blessed. That is divine prosperity.

Divine prosperity is a life you live in blessing humanity and lacking nothing. It's a state of well-being, increase, and stability in every area of your life. When the blessing of the Lord is upon your life, you will succeed where others fail and be accepted where others are rejected. When the blessing of the Lord is upon your life, you will be surrounded with favor as with a shield. (See Psalm 5:12). When the blessing of the Lord is upon you, everything will work together for your good, meaning that circumstances and situations of life that are supposed to bring you down will end up lifting you even higher than where you were. The blessing of the Lord upon your life is what catapults you into great success and prestige in life. When God blesses you, you will excel in what you do and outshine your competitors. You will flourish like the palm tree and grow like the cedar in Lebanon. (See Psalm 92:12).

The blessing of the Lord upon Joseph was what

catapulted him from been a slave boy in Potiphar's house and from the prison-house into the palace, and he became not only the prime minister of ancient Egypt but also the savior of Egypt and a preserver of posterity during the years of famine. The blessing of the Lord gave Joseph supernatural ideas by which he preserved Egypt for the whole years of famine, which was an economic crash in other words, because the Bible says that *money failed in the land of Egypt.* (See Genesis 47:15).

The blessing of the Lord upon your life is what empowers you to enjoy divine prosperity. The blessing of the Lord is that light of God that shines in you, and through you others can light up their own lives. "*God sent a word unto Jacob, and it lighted up all Israel.*" (Isaiah 9:8) The Word of God in you is the light, and it's the *blessing*. The blessing of the Lord is a divine revelation of God's Word to your heart by which you prosper and make others also prosper through you. Divine prosperity is a function of divine revelation, or divine secrets, upon which you operate. This divine revelation or secrets is given only to those who are in Christ. Jesus said: "unto you, it is given to know the mystery of the kingdom of God: but unto them that are without, all these things are done in parables". (Mark 4:11).

Divine revelation or secret comes to you in many forms but in just two ways; horizontal revelation and vertical revelation. The horizontal revelation is when you get a revelation through a direct encounter with an anointed man or woman of God, either by sitting in the same conference room where the anointed man or woman of God is teaching or through his or her books or inspired audio messages. The vertical revelation is when you are taken by the Spirit to see things by yourself in the realm of the spirit. This can happen during some intense fasting and prayer and this kind of revelation is in levels, as we saw in Ezekiel 47:4-6. The apostle Paul explained his experience of this kind of vertical revelation in 2 Corinthians 12:1-4, and also the apostle John in Revelation 6:1-17. The Word of God in your spirit is the seed of God's blessing upon your life. When God wants to bless someone, He sends His Word to that individual. Your ability, therefore, to obediently walk in the light of God's Word that you have received, is what makes the difference.

Some people have the seed of God's Word in their lives, but their blessing is yet to come to limelight because they have not taken the steps in walking in the light of that Word that they have received. That is because to walk in the light of God's Word, which is the blessing of the Lord upon your life, you must go against the general belief system of the world. You must step out of the ways of the world into the ways of the kingdom of God. This is why Christianity is not a religion, it's a life we live by divine revelation, and the revealer is the Holy Spirit of God that dwells in us.

We saw in the Scriptures that David never lost any of the many battles he fought. That was because David always inquires from God before embarking on any battle, and God always responds back to him with divine revelations by which he always obtains victories in battle. Here are just a few verses where David enquired from God:

Then they told David, saying, Behold, the Philistines

fight against Keilah, and they rob the threshingfloors. Therefore David enquired of the Lord, saying, Shall I go and smite these Philistines? And the Lord said unto David, Go, and smite the Philistines, and save Keilah. (1 Samuel 23:1-2).

And David enquired at the Lord, saying, Shall I pursue after this troop? shall I overtake them? And he answered him, Pursue: for thou shalt surely overtake them, and without fail recover all. (1 Samuel 30:8).

And David enquired of the Lord, saying, Shall I go up to the Philistines? wilt thou deliver them into mine hand? And the Lord said unto David, Go up: for I will doubtless deliver the Philistines into thine hand. (2 Samuel 5:19).

And when David enquired of the Lord, he said, Thou shalt not go up; but fetch a compass behind them, and come upon them over against the mulberry trees. (2 Samuel 5:23).

David himself testified that God is the One who taught his hands to war and his fingers to fight so that a bow of steel is broken by his arms.

(See Psalm 18:34, and also Psalm 144:1). You may be asking, how was it possible? The answer is through *divine revelation*. David engaged divine secrets all his life; he never took any step without first enquiring from God. Even when there was a conspiracy in his own palace to dethrone him, the conspiracy failed because David engaged divine secret by which the counsel of the great Ahithophel was turned into foolishness, and the conspiracy failed. (See 2 Samuel 15:30-34, and also 2 Samuel 17:1-14).

When God blessed Solomon with *the knowledge of wisdom* and with enlargement of the heart that made him very wise and wealthy, how did God bless him? The following Scripture told us: *"And God said to Solomon, because this was in thine heart, and thou hast not asked riches, wealth, or honour, nor the life of thine enemies, neither yet hast asked long life; but hast asked wisdom and knowledge for thyself, that thou mayest judge my people, over whom I have made thee king:* **wisdom and knowledge is granted unto thee; and I will give thee riches, and wealth, and honour,** *such as none of the kings have had that have been before thee, neither shall there any after thee have* *the like."* (2 Chronicles 1:11-12). Did you see that? God only spoke words to Solomon, and that settles it. God's Word is all you need to be blessed because in God's Word is the seed of the blessing. Did you also notice that God added wealth, riches, and honor? That is because wisdom and knowledge produce wealth, riches, and honor. (See Proverbs 8:18) As a child of God in Christ, you are eligible to receive that seed of God's Word in your spirit by which you prosper and become a blessing to your world.

When you are a carrier of the blessing of the Lord, anywhere you enter that place will prosper because of you. The blessing of the Lord recognizes no boundaries. This was the experience and testimony of Laban because of Jacob. (See Genesis 30:27). When Joseph arrived in the house of Potiphar as a slave boy, and he was put in charge of all that was in Potiphar' house, the Bible says that *"from the time that he made Joseph overseer in his house and [put him in charge] over all that he owned, **that the Lord blessed the Egyptian's house because of Joseph;** so the Lord's blessing was on everything that Potiphar owned, in the house and in the field."* (Genesis 39:5.

AMP). Also because of Peter, the house of Cornelius received salvation, and they were blessed with the Spirit of God by which they will receive divine revelation to walk in divine prosperity. (Act 10:44).

In the most popular Bible verse on prosperity, which is Deuteronomy 28: 1-14, it began by saying: *"Now it shall be, if you diligently listen to and obey the voice (Word) of the Lord your God, being careful to do all of His commandments which I am commanding you today, the Lord your God will set you high above all the nations of the earth. All these blessings will come upon you and overtake you if you pay attention to the voice (Word) of the Lord your God."*(verse 2 AMP). Did you notice that the *Voice or Word* came twice in the first two verses of this chapter? That is because the seed of the blessing is in God's Word, and you must apply, in your own personal life, what the Word says. That is the gateway to walking in divine prosperity, the Word of God.

• *Walking in Divine Prosperity*

To walk in divine prosperity, you must understand the platform and its terms. In the previous section, we have defined and detailed divine prosperity for your understanding. So in this section, you will be learning the platform and the terms of divine prosperity so that you can engage yourself with it and start prospering for the glory of Christ.

What then, is the platform for divine prosperity? And how can I engage myself with it? Good question; the platform for divine prosperity is *sacrifice*. The platform is the altar of sacrifice where you sacrifice yourself. You may be asking what it means to sacrifice yourself. It means living for others and not for yourself. It's where you offer yourself for the destruction of selfishness, covetousness, and greed. The altar is where you destroy all the desires and longings of the flesh and surrender to the will of the Spirit. Carnality is the enemy of divine prosperity. Until carnality is dealt with in the altar of sacrifice, divine prosperity is not in view. This is why Jesus said: *"Verily, verily, I say unto you, except a corn of wheat fall into the ground and dies, it abideth alone: but if it dies, it bringeth forth much fruit."* (John 12:24).

As I've said, divine prosperity is in the platform of spirituality, which is living according to the revelations of Scriptures as revealed to you by the Spirit from time to time. But until carnality is destroyed, divine revelations are far from you, and without divine revelation, how can you walk in divine prosperity. If you refuse to die like the *corn of wheat*, how can you spring up and produce much fruits? Do you know that baptism unto Christ means dying and resurrecting with a new life? Therefore as a new creature in Christ, you are dead unto carnality and alive unto righteousness. So you must accept your new creature status and consciously walk in it. That is what I mean by sacrifice. The Scripture declares that: "you are to think of yourselves as dead, so far as sin(carnality) is concerned, but living in fellowship with God through Christ Jesus." (Romans 6:11. GNT).

You must accept the fact that you are dead to the ways of the world (carnality) and that you are now living in the ways of God through Christ.

That is what the above Scripture is saying. There are Christians who have not yet accepted their new creation status and are not consciously walking in it. Such Christians deny themselves the benefits of salvation, which comes by practical application of divine revelation, which they can only receive by walking in the Spirit. Carnality makes you powerless. It robs you off the power to command things. It frustrates your ability to distinguish between the voice of your flesh and the voice of God. Carnality makes you operate in the realms of men instead of the sphere of the Spirit. It makes you think and talk the same way the world thinks and talks.

There are Christians who never go into fasting and prayer. They don't have time to read their Bibles and meditate on God's Word. You cannot be surfeiting every time and expect to walk in divine revelation. It doesn't work that way. Some Christians eat and overeat everything they see without even checking the content value of what they eat. Most of the diseases that people are suffering from are traceable to the junk foods they eat on a daily basis without knowing it. Salvation has been giving to you in Christ, but according to the Scriptures in Philippians 2:12, you are the person to work out your salvation. Health, healing, prosperity, peace of God, protection, success, just name it, everything has been given to you in salvation, but you must work it out yourself.

The fact that you are reading this book is proof that you desire to know how to walk in the light of divine peace, prosperity, and security, and that is precisely what I'm sharing with you here as the Lord has placed in my heart. Christians who received the package of salvation in Christ and never cared to know what it takes to maximize the blessings of salvation may only make it to heaven, but their lives here on earth will be frustrated by the forces of darkness of this world. That is why you must make up your mind now to walk in the light of what is being shared with you in this book and recommend it to your family members and fellow Christians within your reach. Spirituality is the only remedy for carnality. Just as you operate your new mobile device to utilize its features, you must work out your own salvation to enjoy the best of the blessings of salvation. This is why Jesus said:

"Let your light so shine before men, that they may see your good works, and glorify your Father which is in heaven." (Matthew 5:16). You must let the light of your salvation shine. Notice He said, *let your light shine*, meaning that you are the one to make it happen, and what I'm sharing with you in this book will get you started in letting your light shine. The shining of your light is divine prosperity speaking in the lives of many around the world.

As a child of God in Christ, you are eligible for divine revelation by which you walk in divine prosperity. But you have to make it happen. Divine revelation doesn't just pop up like that. You must be in the spirit to receive divine revelation. Spirituality, as I have said, is living according to the teachings of Christ. It means living a life of Biblical principles. That is what makes you spiritual as a Christian, and that is also what empowers you to receive divine revelation by which you prosper and become a blessing to your world because the seed of God's blessing is in His Word, which is divine revelation. You must also understand that divine revelation is triggered by Scriptures. If you are bankrupt of the knowledge of Scriptures, you will also be bankrupt of divine revelation, and without divine revelation, your prosperity is not in view. We can as well say that Scriptures are the gateways to divine revelation. That is why the Bible says: *"The entrance (unfolding) of God's words giveth light; it giveth understanding unto the simple."* (Psalm 119:130). It means that the knowledge of the Logos and Rhema of Scriptures is what produces divine revelation and understanding by which you command divine prosperity. You must be a voracious student of Scriptures, which is the only way you can flow in divine revelation and command divine prosperity all around.

Now, what is divine revelation? Divine revelation is a secret knowledge that God reveals to you by His Spirit. It can be the knowledge of an invention that will bless humanity and prosper you financially. It can also be the knowledge of how to improve something that is already in use for better services and usability. Divine revelation can be the knowledge of how to prevent something unpleasant from happening, like in the case of Joseph, who, by divine revelation, advised the king on how to escape the famine in Egypt. (See Genesis

41:33-45). It was by divine revelation that Jacob produced the speckled and spotted animals by which he prospered. (See Genesis 30:37-43). It was also by divine revelation that David acquired massive wealth, strategized the defeat of all his enemies, and won in all the battles he fought as Israel's king. By divine revelation, Isaac remained in the land of the Philistines when he wanted to go to Egypt, and he became so prosperous in the land of the Philistines that the people of Philistines envied him. (See Genesis 26:1-14).

Most of the inventions that have added value to humanity and solved human problems of all kinds are products of divine revelation, like the inventions of Michael Faraway, as we saw briefly in the previous section. We have read about great inventors who never completed the normal school years, but through divine revelation, they invented things that have blessed humanity in diverse ways. Thomas Edison, the inventor of the light bulb, the motion picture camera, phonograph, and more, spent only three months in High School. It was his mother who taught him how to read and write after he was expelled from school because the teachers thought he could not learn.

Orville and Wilbur Wright, known as the Wright Brothers, invented the flying machine and flew the first airplane, having never graduated from Hign School. Larry Ellison, Founder of Oracle Corporation and one of the world's wealthiest people, spent only one year at the University of Chicago. Michael Dell, Founder of Dell Corporation, also spent only one year at the University of Texas and has contributed significantly to the computer industry. Steve Jobs, the founder of Apple Inc, spent only one year at Reed College. He introduced the Macintosh and is recognized as one of the pioneers of the computer revolution. His many visionary creations, such as the iPad and iPhone, have changed the lives of millions of people.

That is just a few of the list of individuals who operated by divine revelation after having dropped out of school. Without divine revelation, the whole world wouldn't have known anything at all like civilization. The by-products of divine revelation are what have empowered schools to properly educate the human minds for analytical and critical thinking so that knowledge of inventions can be applied correctly for the benefit of humanity. But today, the enemy has corrupted and has taken over many schools around the world, and a lot of people have been miss-educated. The knowledge of inventions has now been misapplied across nations. That is why the world is getting more and more unsafe by the day because knowledge is being applied in the wrong direction. Falsehood, deception, and inventions of weapons of mass destruction of all kinds have become the order of the day. The enemy is gradually leading humanity into self-destruct by miss-education; therefore, the only antidote for this miss-education plan of the enemy is the teachings of Christ, which is the Word of God that smashes rocks into pieces as the Scripture declares: *"Is not my Word like as a fire? saith the Lord; and like a hammer that breaketh the rock in pieces"*. (Jeremiah 23:29). Go after the Word of God so that you can be divinely inspired and guided to manifest prosperity in your life and become a blessing to humanity.

To walk in divine revelation, you must be a man or a woman of a highly disciplined mind. Set out some days in every month to go into fasting and prayer, coupled with intense study of the Bible and other great anointed books. And as you engage in this exercise, pay attention to spontaneous thoughts, dreams, flashes of pictures in your mind and the *still small voice* in your heart, because these are the channels through which God speaks to us. However, you must cross-check your revelations on the platform of peace to ensure they are from God. If you have any revelation without the peace of God in your spirit, then it's not from God, for God speaks to us with peace, and peace is our guide and guard in Christ. It's our umpire that confirms and settles things for us. (See Psalm 85:8, Philippians 4:7, and Colossians 3:15).

Avoid noise and make your home as noiseless as possible. The voice of the Spirit, as I've said, is a *still small voice*, and sometimes it comes as a spontaneous flash of thought in your mind, so you must always have calmness of mind and with quiet environment to pick up the voice of the Spirit. Also, you must always maintain a positive mindset and an attitude of faith. Avoid negative minded people. Always be happy and joyful. Eat less and exercise more to maintain physical fitness and also avoid dizzy feelings that come as a result of fatty foods in the stomach. Eating less and exercising more makes you look younger and is also very good for health and longevity in general.

Celebrate life every day with your family and friends. Always look for something to appreciate God for and be thankful to Him all the time. Remain a learner by reading at least one good book every week. Avoid anyone or anything that causes you to be unhappy and upset. Are you an introvert who likes to maintain solo? Good, but you must master the art of networking with like-minded individuals to broaden up your perspectives. (For more on Networking see chapter three of my book; Mastering The Forces of Success). What I'm sharing with you here is how to flow in divine revelation through which you will manifest divine prosperity and become a blessing to humanity.

Don't watch what you don't want. The world is full of negativity, and the media is not helping the matter at all. Use the most powerful senses of your body to project positivity and success into your mind. You can do this by training yourself always to see positive, hear positive, and talk positive. The most potent senses of your body are your eyes (the sense of sight), your ears (the sense of hearing), and your mouth (the sense of taste). The Scripture says: **"the light of the body is the eye**: *if therefore thine eye be single, thy whole body shall be full of light."* (Matthew 6:22), about your ears, the Scripture declares: *"faith cometh by hearing, and hearing by the Word of God."* (Romans 10:17), and about your mouth, the Scripture says: *"Death and life are in the power of the tongue."* (Proverbs 18:21). You must discipline yourself in what you watch, what you hear, and what you say with your mouth daily. What you see and what you hear determines how you think, and also forms the words you speak. Therefore you cannot afford to watch and listen to all the negative news on the media if you want to flow in divine revelation.

Great men and women, both past and present, who have significantly contributed to the advancement and development of humanity, were individuals with highly disciplined minds. They control what they see, hear, and say with their mouths because they understood that negative influences on the mind via the eyes, the ears, and the mouth chokes the Word and blocks the flow of divine revelation. (See Mark 4:19).

Studies have shown that visuals and audios are the two most powerful ways by which one can put to sleep the rational mind, which is the conscious mind, and project ideas directly into the human subconscious. And if the ideas are negative, it will negatively affect every area of that person's life, including the blockage of the flow of divine revelation, without which divine prosperity is not in view, because light and darkness cannot co-exist.

Studies have also shown that the subconscious mind does not know the difference between that which is imagined and that which is real. So what you hear and see repeatedly is automatically accepted as real by the subconscious mind, and it goes to work to make it a real-life experience for you because the subconscious mind has the power to turn your mindset into a real-life experience.

It takes your seed of thought and turns it into a harvest of real life experience. That is why ads are repeated multiple times daily on different platforms because the companies know that once the subconscious mind accepts the idea displayed via the ads, that is if you are exposed to the ads, you will be led subconsciously to purchase the product or services advertised, even if you do not really need it. Ignorance of this fact is the reason why a lot of people fail in life generally because they allow themselves to be exposed to negative influences, and while desiring success on the conscious level, they experience the opposite, due to the negative influences or suggestions they have repeatedly given to their subconscious minds unawares.

Now you can understand why you must always focus only on God's Word and on things that add value to your life daily and inspires you for creativity and maximization of your potential. You must engage your mind on things that will lift your spirit and boost your faith. Michael Faraday operated on divine revelation through intense study of Scriptures and scientific books, and he became one of the most outstanding scientists in history. If he had accepted his poor background and spent his time on useless things, do you think he would have become what he became? Of course not, wisdom said; *"blessed is the man that heareth me, watching daily at my gates, waiting at the posts of my doors."* (Proverbs 8: 34). You cannot be *watching* daily at the gates and *waiting* at the doorposts of wisdom (God's Word) and not be blessed. You can't be watching TV all day and be browsing on social media to check out the latest gossips and the latest this and that, and at the end of the day, you expect to flow in divine revelation, no sir, it doesn't work that way.

Thomas Edison, after his mother taught him how to read and write, immersed himself into an intense study of books by which he was inspired to numerous inventions that have brought light and life to humanity. Wake up. No matter your age, you are not getting younger; rather you are getting older as the day passes. Even if you are only 20 years old, you can positively change the world for God's glory. Mark Zuckerberg was only 19 years old when he founded Facebook in 2004. We also saw in the Scriptures that; *"Sixteen years old was*

Uzziah when he began to reign, and he reigned fifty and two years in Jerusalem. His mother's name also was Jecoliah of Jerusalem. And he did that which was right in the sight of the Lord, according to all that his father Amaziah did. And he sought God in the days of Zechariah, who had understanding in the visions of God: and as long as he sought the Lord, God made him to prosper". (2 Chronicles 26:3-5).

What did you see in that scripture? You may have noticed that Uzziah was a teenager when he began to lead as a king. But what I saw is the secret behind his prosperity, which says that **he sought God in the days of Zechariah, who had understanding in the visions of God: and as long as he sought the Lord, God made him prosper**. (verse 5). Meaning that Uzziah sought God through someone who had a greater understanding in the things or ways of God, and by that, God gave him a divine revelation through which he prospered. That is spiritual mentorship. That is what you do when you read books written by anointed men and women of God, such as the one you are reading now. You can never find any true success that is not traceable to divine revelation via the Word of God. If you sight carnality, run for your life. Carnality is a destiny killer and vision destroyer. It has destroyed many without them knowing it. It has made many to only exist without living. Spirituality, which is living according to the teachings of Christ, is the way to fulfill destiny in a ground style.

As you begin to flow in divine revelation after reading this book, and start enjoying divine prosperity and becoming a blessing to your world, it's imperative to watch out for pride. Pride is an enemy that never surrenders. The more you prosper, the more you should humble yourself and watch out for pride. Pride has destroyed a lot of great successful people, both past and present. It takes the grace and mercy of God to escape pride when one has achieved great success in life. Pride makes you think that you are civilized and that you can do anything. Pride turns people into fools who say in their hearts that there is no God, all in the same of civilization. (See Psalm 14:14). You must always acknowledge God and give Him all the glory, no matter your level of achievement.

Never support any course that does not bring

glory and honor to the name of Christ. Never put your wealth in any medical research or experiment that will plague humanity with decease so that you can sell the antidote as vaccines to get richer. That is what many have done, and they brought the curse of God upon themselves and their families. They secretly use the blessing of God upon their lives to sponsor and promote the agenda of the devil in this world. That is the highest sin that God never forgives.

King Solomon ended up with pride against God when he began building temples and shrines for the gods of this world, and the Scripture declares: *"For Solomon went after Ashtoreth the goddess of the Zidonians, and after Milcom the abomination of the Ammonites. And Solomon did evil in the sight of the Lord, and went not fully after the Lord, as did David his father. Then did Solomon build an high place for Chemosh, the abomination of Moab, in the hill that is before Jerusalem, and for Molech, the abomination of the children of Ammon. And likewise did he for all his strange wives, which burnt incense and sacrificed unto their gods.*

And the Lord was angry with Solomon, because his heart was turned from the Lord God of Israel, which had appeared unto him twice, And had commanded him concerning this thing, that he should not go after other gods: but he kept not that which the Lord commanded. Wherefore the Lord said unto Solomon, Forasmuch as this is done of thee, and thou hast not kept my covenant and my statutes, which I have commanded thee, I will surely rend the kingdom from thee, and will give it to thy servant".(1 Kings 11:1-25).

King Uzziah also ended up with pride against God, and a group of priests tried to warn him, but he didn't listen because of the pride of wealth, power, and influence, and the Lord cursed him. See how he ended up as the Scripture declares: *"But when he was strong, **his heart was lifted up to his destruction**: for he transgressed against the Lord his God, and went into the temple of the Lord to burn incense upon the altar of incense.....And Uzziah the king was a leper unto the day of his death, and dwelt in a several house, being a leper; for he was cut off from the house of the Lord: and Jotham his son was over the king's house, judging the people of the land".(2 Chronicles 26:16-21).*

There were many kings in the Bible that God prospered mightily and enormously, but they ended up with pride against God, and God cursed them. Some of them died on the battlefield due to God's anger against them. Like King Ahab; (See 1 Kings 22:29-38). Also, King Saul ended up with pride, and God departed from him, and he took his own life on a battlefield. (See 1 Samuel 31:1-7).

Ahithophel, one of King David's counselors, was a man whom God blessed abundantly with wisdom and extraordinary insight. The Bible says that the counsel of Ahithophel was as the counsel of God Himself (see 2 Samuel 16:23). But he ended up with pride against God by supporting Absalom against David, the Lord's anointed, and God turned against him by overriding his advise and turned it into foolishness, and the mighty Ahithophel went and took his own life. (See 2 Samuel 17:23). That is the reason you hear most of the time about billionaires and multimillion-aires who died mysteriously or committed suicide. Such death shows that the person is under a spiritual curse because the Scripture says: *"Thus saith the Lord; Cursed be the man that trusteth in man, and maketh flesh his arm, and whose heart departeth from the Lord."* (Jeremiah 17:5).

There are many projects and causes around the world that glorify God and honors the name of Jesus Christ. Look for such places and put your money there. You cannot sponsor and promote ungodly and wicked practices of this world with the wealth God has given you. That is evil in the eyes of God but many do not know it. If you read the Scriptures very well, you will see this mystery in the lives of many great kings whom God empowered to prosper. Only a few of them escaped this deadly weapon of the enemy, pride!

Moses warned the Israelites about this deadly weapon of the enemy because Moses understood very well the consequences of this on anyone whose heart is lifted against God in pride after having been blessed by God. He said; *"Beware that thou forget not the Lord thy God, in not keeping his commandments, and his judgments, and his statutes, which I command thee this day: Lest when thou hast eaten and art full, and hast built goodly houses, and dwelt therein; And when thy herds and thy flocks mul-*

tiply, and thy silver and thy gold is multiplied, and all that thou hast is multiplied; Then thine heart be lifted up, and thou forget the Lord thy God, which brought thee forth out of the land of Egypt, from the house of bondage". (Deuteronomy 8:11-13).

Did you see how important Moses thought it was to warn them about this? Now let me shock you with verse 19 of the same chapter; *"And it shall be, if thou do at all forget the Lord thy God, and walk after other gods, and serve them, and worship them, I testify against you this day that YE SHALL SURELY PERISH."* (Deuteronomy 8:19). Pride is the weapon the devil has been using since time immemorial to bring down mighty men. May you never fall for pride in Jesus name! You will prosper, and you will sponsor and promote God's kingdom and causes that will bring glory and honor to the name of Jesus Christ, and your wealth and blessing will continue to speak generations after.

Finally, and most importantly, to walk in divine prosperity, you must master the art of giving. Giving opens up the windows of heaven for you to receive an abundant blessing (divine revelation) by which you prosper exceedingly. Giving increases your capacity and credibility to receive more and more divine revelation by which you prosper beyond expectation. When you give for the glory of God in acknowledgment of His sovereignty over all, the enemy is automatically and divinely banned and prohibited from touching you, your family, and anything that has to do with you on the earth. That is what we call divine exemption, and it's on the platform of giving. It's also the mystery of the famous Scripture that says: *"Bring ye all the tithes into the storehouse, that there may be meat in mine house, and prove me now herewith, saith the Lord of hosts, if I will not open you the windows of heaven, and pour you out a blessing, that there shall not be room enough to receive it. And I will rebuke the devourer for your sakes, and he shall not destroy the fruits of your ground; neither shall your vine cast her fruit before the time in the field, saith the Lord of hosts. And all nations shall call you blessed: for ye shall be a delightsome land, saith the Lord of hosts"*. (Malachi 3:10-12).

That is a compelling command through which a believer can experience immense and overflowing prosperity through divine revelation or ideas.

But a lot of Christians don't know this. When they read this Scripture, they seem to picture money falling from the sky. But God is not primarily talking about money here; rather, God is saying that by honoring Him with your tithe, He will open **for you** the windows of heaven (**divine access**) and pour you out a blessing (**divine revelation**). Through this divine revelation, you will prosper financially beyond measure because you will acquire lots of money through the service or services you are rendering via the divine revelation at your disposal. Also, He will cause favor to come on you from every angle. People will favor you financially and patronize your businesses and righteous endeavors. All nations will call you bless because you will be outstanding in the entire globe for God's glory.

You must also understand that the purpose of God's blessing upon your life is first for His kingdom and service to humanity through divine revelation. And divine revelation, as we have seen, can be a piece of knowledge on how to invent something that can solve a human problem of some kind, or improve existing products or services for more excellent human value and impact. Divine revelation can also mean a supernatural increase in your trading business or promotion in your place of work. Then, as you now prosper financially and otherwise through divine revelation, God expects you to honor Him by giving ten percent of your income to the church for the preaching of the gospel of Christ to the world. The gospel is for a witness to the world. (See Matthew 24:14). So that at Christ's return, no one will have any excuse for not being saved, and since God does not wish that all men should perish, the gospel must continue to be preached to save as many as possible before Christ returns.

Therefore, you must master the art of giving for the glory of Christ by supporting ministries and ministers of the gospel of Christ to take the gospel of salvation to the ends of the world. As the Lord prospers you, begin with your local church, and then gradually extend to other churches globally where the name of Christ is honored, and the gospel of Christ is preached. I'm a tireless giver. Not only to the church of my fathers in the Lord, but also to other churches, because I'm not the only person God has sent to preach the gospel to the world, and by giving, my capacity and credibility for more blessings are enlarged. Be a tireless giver, and don't ever stop giving for the glory of Christ. As you do this, you will see the hand of God lifting you higher in every area of your life with more and more divine revelation for more and more enjoyment of divine prosperity.

Also, as you get richer by the day, extend your giving by setting up a foundation for orphanages and older people who have *no one but God through you to help them.* Invest in Godly education for these children and let them become a light to the world through the blessing of God in your life. Give no room for pride. Don't finance any coup d'état to overthrow a government and install puppet one. Don't invest in corrupt dealings to misappropriate state or national funds, and don't support or sponsor any cause that is against the ordinances of God upon the earth. All these are what many have done and continue to do with the wealth God has blessed them with, and they have brought curses on themselves. Divine judgment awaits them if they don't repent and start doing the right thing.

You are a chosen treasure of God. The enemy will not succeed in manipulating you with pride to misuse the blessings of God upon your life. Mercy and grace are on your side. Angels will fight your battles, and the victory is yours to the glory of Christ. Your wealth will be a limitless wealth and vast in generational impact. You have just received into your hands the keys to walking in divine prosperity. Now go and prosperity without limit!

Three

The Wisdom of Divine Security

THE WISDOM OF DIVINE SECURITY

He that dwelleth in the secret place of the most High shall abide under the shadow of the Almighty. (Psalm 91:1).

Lack of knowledge of the wisdom of divine security is the reason many are living their lives under the fear of one thing or another. Especially after hearing the bad news on the media every day about man's ungodly activities across nations, resulting into bomb explosions, mass shootings, people losing money through man-made stock market crash, an outbreak of a virus, an episode of a political or religious clash, etc. All this news on the media is part of the enemy's devices to make human beings afraid because, without fear, there is no way he can control the world.

However, fear is a product of ignorance. If you are bankrupt of God's Word, you will always be afraid even when there is actually nothing to be afraid of. The Scripture says: *"there were they in great* *fear, **where no fear was**: for God hath scattered the bones of him that encampeth against thee: thou hast put them to shame, because God hath despised them."* (Psalm 53:5). God defeated the enemy by the death of Christ more than two thousand years ago. The only weapon the enemy is using against humanity is fear; therefore, until you are afraid, the enemy is powerless. It's fear in your mind that empowers the enemy. Refuse to be afraid because there is absolutely nothing to be afraid of.

Again, fear is a product of ignorance, and the reason the enemy is blinding minds about the gospel of Christ, according to 2 Corinthians 4:4, is because he knows that if you have the knowledge of the wisdom of God at your disposal, you will not fall for his lies and tricks. If you don't buy into his lies and deceits, you cannot be afraid, and without fear, he cannot control you. That is why Paul the apostle, said: *"lest Satan should get an advantage of us: **for we are not ignorant of his devices."*** (2 Corinthians 2:11). To be ignorant of the devices of the enemy means that you are bankrupt of God's Word because the Word of God reveals the instruments of the enemy to you so that you can always uncover the lies of the enemy and shatter his plans into pieces. Ignorance is the power of the enemy to control and rule over lives in this world. The knowledge of the wisdom of God is Truth, and by walking in the light of Truth, the power of the enemy is broken, and you are set free. That is what Jesus meant when He said: *"you shall know the truth and the truth shall make you free."* (John 8:32).

For example, someone who used to be a police officer can still harass and intimidate you if you are not aware that he has been expelled from the police force. But if you are aware that he is no longer a police officer and he tries to intimidate you claiming to be a police officer, you will resist him by all means and even call the cops to get him arrested for impersonation. What I'm saying here is that as a child of God in Christ, you must have the knowledge of the wisdom of God operating in your life in its totality. We are commanded to *"Let the words of Christ dwell (tabernacle) in us richly in all wisdom."* (Colossians 3:16). The knowledge of the wisdom of God operating mightily in your life frustrates the plans and purposes of the enemy. It makes you untouchable, and you can undertake to use the knowledge of the wisdom of God at your disposal to set free as many as possible those whose lives are being ruled and controlled by the devices of the enemy.

Divine security, therefore, is all about dwelling in the secret place of the Highest. This secret place, where the enemy has no access, this secret place, where the shadow of the Almighty becomes your covering, is where divine security is found. My job, therefore, in this chapter, is to show you the practical ways of dwelling in the secret place so that you can abide under the shadow of the Almighty.

Martin Luther King Jr. said: *"The greatest enemy of knowledge is not ignorance; it is the illusion of knowledge."* The illusion of knowledge means to think that you know what you do not know, and then when circumstances arise that require you to apply the knowledge that you thought you know, you then realize that you really do not know that which you thought you knew. That is the problem with a lot of Christians all over the world. They only have shallow knowledge of the Scriptures but lack the revelation behind it. They read only the letters, but they are not in touch with *the Spirit behind the letters*. Therefore when challenging issues arise that requires Rhema to handle, they start shaking in fear. That is the illusion of knowledge.

Therefore, in this chapter, I will be leading you once again, to the understanding of what divine security is and how to start walking in it for the glory of God.

• *Understanding Divine Security*

Divine security is about dwelling consistently in the secret place of the Most High God, His Presence. Once you dwell in the secret place, you come automatically under the covering of His shadow. When you are under the shadow of the Almighty, nothing dares you because anything that dares you dares God, and since nothing can dare God, it means you become untouchable.

Divine security is that state where you are not afraid of what man can do because you know who you are and in Whose Presence you stand. Divine security is a state of vibrant and robust health where you or anyone in your family does not get sick. *"And the inhabitant shall not say, I am sick: the people that dwell therein shall be forgiven their iniquity"*. (Isaiah 33:24).

As I write, I remember six to seven years ago when I used to get sick with fever and severe headaches often. But in the year 2014, it dawned on me by divine revelation as I was meditating on Matthew 8:17 and suddenly, bam, the light hit my heart, that as a child of God in Christ, I'm not supposed to be sick and lying in a hospital bed, because **Himself took my infirmities, and bare my sicknesses.** I grasped that revelation, and I began to walk in the light of it with great faith in my spirit. It has been more than six years now, and I have not had any health issues, and not even any member of my family has ever had any health issues since then. That is what happens when you dwell consistently in the Presence of God. He covers you and everything that is connected to you. The Scripture also declares: *"Thou wilt show me the path of life: in thy presence is fullness of joy; at thy right hand there are pleasures forevermore."* (Psalm 16:11). It means that in the Presence of God, first He shows you (divine revelation) how to live a good life, and then you experience the fullness of joy and pleasure forevermore, and then His shadow covers not only your health and wealth but everything that concerns you. (See Psalm 138:8).

Divine security is an exemption from the attacks of the enemy against humanity. When Jacob came to live in Egypt after Joseph has become the second man in command, they were given a land called Goshen to live in. Then many years later, the land of Goshen became a city vastly populated by Jacob's descendants. And then during the Exodus, when all kinds of plagues began to hit Egypt, the land of Goshen was exempted as the Scripture declares: "*and the hail struck throughout the whole land of Egypt, all that was in the field, both man and beast; and the hail struck every herb of the field and broke every tree of the field. **Only in the land of Goshen, where the children of Israel were, there was no hail**"*. (Exodus 9:24-26). That is divine security because God is a covenant-keeping God from generation to generation. When you dwell in the secret place of the Most High, which is the Presence of God, everything harmful and contrary to the divine plan of God for your life will be running away from you.

Heavy hail, accompanied by fire, were falling on everything and everyone in Egypt, exempt in the land of Goshen. That is because the people dwelling in Goshen have a covenant of exemption with God through Abraham, whose child you also are in Christ, for the Scripture declares: **"Now we, brethren, as Isaac was, are the children of promise."**

(Galatians 4:28). When you dwell in the secret place, which is the Presence of God, the oppressions of the wicked in this world will not come near you. When they see you coming, they will disappear because the Scripture tells us that *"The sea saw it, and fled: Jordan was driven back. The mountains skipped like rams, and the little hills like lambs. What ailed thee, O thou sea, that thou fleddest? thou Jordan, that thou wast driven back? Ye mountains, that ye skipped like rams; and ye little hills, like lambs? Tremble, thou earth,* **at the Presence of the Lord**, at **the Presence of the God of Jacob**; *Which turned the rock into a standing water, the flint into a fountain of waters"*. (Psalm 114:3-8).

The secret place, which is the glorious Presence of God, is not in any geographical location. Don't let anyone tell you that you can meet God by going to so and so mountain or place. Our fathers went up to the hill, yes, but today the Presence of God is no longer in the mountain. The Shekinah glory also is no longer in the holy of holies made with hands. Jesus told the Samaritan woman at the well, *"Woman, believe Me, a time is coming [when God's kingdom comes] when you will worship the Father nei-*

ther on this mountain nor in Jerusalem." (John 4:21. AMP). Today the kingdom of God is here, which is the body of Christ, believers all over the world. So the issue of going to the mountain or in Jerusalem to worship God no longer applies. Also, on the day Christ died victoriously on the cross, the Scripture declares that "*the veil [of the Holy of Holies] of the temple was torn in two from top to bottom; the earth shook and the rocks were split apart*". (Matthew 27:51. AMP). That means God's Presence is also no longer in the holy of holies because the Scripture also declares: "*but into the second [inner tabernacle, the Holy of Holies], only the high priest enters and then only once a year, and never without bringing a sacrifice of blood, which he offers as a substitutionary atonement for himself and for the sins of the people. **By this the Holy Spirit signifies that the way into the Holy Place [the true Holy of Holies and the Presence of God] has not yet been disclosed as long as the first or outer tabernacle is still standing** [that is, as long as the Levitical system of worship remains a recognized institution*". (Hebrews 9:7-8. AMP).

What we are dealing with here is that the earthly holy of holies was only a shadow for the true Holy of Holies, which is heavenly. Christ, by His own blood through the death on the cross, entered into the true Holy of Holies not made with human hands and in the Presence of God for us, therefore making the way open for us to be in the Presence of God with Him and in Him as our High Priest. *"For Christ is not entered into the holy places made with hands, which are the figures of the true; but into heaven itself, now to appear in the presence of God for us."* (Hebrews 9:24). The Presence of God is now in us. We are now in the Presence of God because we are in Christ and only those who are in Christ can experience or dwell in the very glorious Presence of the Father. *"Let us, therefore, come boldly to the throne of grace, that we may obtain mercy and find grace to help in time of need."* (Hebrews 4:16). Where is the throne of grace? The Presence of God, and why did he say come with boldness? Because the enemy has lied that you cannot come to God's Presence because you are a sinner, but that is the main reason Paul the apostle uses the Word boldness because it's by coming boldly to the throne of grace that you obtain mercy and be saved. *"For by grace are ye saved through faith, and that not of yourselves: it is the gift of God."* (Ephesians 2:8). As you come boldly, you did not only obtain mercy and find grace; you remain in the Presence of God because His Presence is now your dwelling place. Jesus said: *"all that the Father giveth me shall come to me; and him that cometh to me I will in no wise cast out."* (John 6:37). Therefore the Presence of God becomes your dwelling place where you abide under His shadow.

Since God's Presence is now in us who are in Christ, it means that you, the reader, recreated in Christ, is a carrier of God's Presence. God is light (See 1 John 1:5), and since darkness can't stand light, then darkness must bow down and clear off the way when you appear because you carry the Presence of God who is light. Elisha operated in this reality when he said: *"As the Lord of hosts liveth, **before whom I stand**"* (1 Kings 18:15). Even Elisha walked in this revelation, how much more you that is in Christ, *"Who obtained a more excellent ministry, the mediator of a better covenant, established upon better promises"*. (See Hebrews 8:6-13). The reason many Christians are going through some unpleasant circumstances in their lives is that they lack the consciousness of the Presence of the Omnipresent in their lives. Like I said earlier, Christianity is a life we live by revelation. That also means that the level of our enjoyment of the benefits of salvation, apart from going to heaven, is mostly determined by the level of divine revelation at our possession.

There was a man called Enoch in Genesis 5:24 who was translated to heaven without death. The Scripture declares that before he was translated into heaven, he testified by faith that he pleased God. (See Hebrews 11:5). Do you know what it means for a man to say he pleased God? In other words, Enoch meant that God has nothing against him. Enoch was so conscious of the Presence of God that God decided to take him up to heaven without letting him see death. The secret place is the Presence of the Omnipresent. Once you are there, you are one hundred and one percent covered and protected from the wickedness of this world. Even when a thousand and ten thousand are falling both at your side and at your right hand, they shall not come near you, because you are in His Presence. (See Psalm 91:7). You must understand who you are and in Whose Presence you stand. That is what I'm talking about here. Jesus said that among all born of women, no one is greater than John the Baptist, but the least person in the Kingdom of God is greater than John. (See Matthew 11:11). Even the splendor of Solomon cannot be compared with the glory we have in Christ, because *"a greater than Solomon is here"* (Matthew 12:42*)*. That Scripture refers to Christ Himself and you are in Christ, meaning that your glory and splendor in salvation is greater than that of Solomon (See Luke 12:27). Wake up and begin to walk in the light of who you are in Christ.

When you begin to walk in the light of who you are and in Whose Presence you stand, you will begin to command signs and wonders, and things will begin to answer at your command. Fear of all kinds will vanish. You will become bold and strong like a lion, always walking majestically and afraid of none. (See Proverbs 30:30). You will become so intimidating that when fear sees you, *fear will become afraid and flee.* When you dwell in the secret place, you are protected from any hidden dangers and from all the deadly diseases that the enemy attacks humanity with. *"surely he shall deliver thee from the snare of the fowler, and from the noisome pesti-lence."* (Psalm 91:3). You will not be afraid of any danger at night or sudden attacks from the enemy during the day or the plagues that strike the world from time to time. (See Psalm 91:4-6).

The Presence of God is a consuming fire that consumes anything that is against your life in God. So when you dwell in His Presence, which is the secret place, you are surrounded by the consuming fire of God that consumes the activities of the mystery of iniquity of this world. (See 2 Thessalonians 2:7). The Presence of God fortifies your spirit, soul, and body, and makes you impenetrable and unreachable by the devices of the enemy. *"There shall no evil befall thee, neither shall any plague come nigh thy dwelling."* (Psalm 91:10). By dwelling in the secret place of the Most High, you become a priority for the services of the angels of His Presence. (See Psalm 91:11-12). When you dwell in the Presence of God, the words you speak in prayers will be confirmed even before you know it. (See Acts 10:44).

The Presence of God was the secret behind Israel's victories during the Exodus, and the Scripture declares that the countries became afraid of them. (See Joshua 6:1, and 2 Chronicles 20:29). That is what happens when you dwell in the Presence of God, which is the secret place of the Most High. In Psalm 51:11, David prayed that God should not cast him away from His Presence because David understood that without the Presence of God in his life, he would become a prey to his enemies. The consciousness of the Presence of God in your life is what makes you a god before men. The manifestations of your divinity are the workings of His Presence in your life.

Moses was a man who enjoyed the Presence of God. Most of his conversations with God were a direct face to face conversation with Elohim Himself. (See Numbers 12:1-8). At a time, Moses was telling God that he will not proceed any further with the Israelites if His Presence not go with them. (See Exodus 33:14-16). Moses said that because he also knew, just like you are knowing now through this book, that without the Presence of the Omnipresent in their midst, they would be defeated by their enemies as they journeyed to the promised land. Your promise land is the fulfillment of your great destiny loaded with vibrant health, abundant wealth, and blessing to humanity. So you must always dwell in His Presence for that great destiny of yours to be fulfilled for the glory of Christ.

The Presence of God guarantees longevity over your life and makes you enjoy the benefits of salvation limitlessly. When you dwell in the Presence of God, you experience divine favor in everything you do, and in every area of your life. *"For thou, Lord, will bless the righteous; and with favour wilt thou compass him as with a shield."* (Psalm 5:12).

We shall now proceed to the next section of this chapter, which is also the last section of this book, and there, you will be ushered into the knowledge of how you can practically walk in divine security.

• *Walking In Divine Security*

We have established so far that, as a child of God in Christ, the Presence of The Omnipresent in your life is what guarantees divine security in everything you do and in every area of your life. However, you must understand how to practically maintain the Presence of God in your life, so that you can always walk in divine security. A lot of Christians don't know this, which is why they are low in current as if they are not Christians. Note that we are warned not to quench the Spirit (See 1 Thessalonians 5:19). This warning indicates that the Spirit can be quenched or, in other words, you are to ensure that the Spirit, which is the fire, the Presence of the Omnipresent in you, is ever burning. It also stands to reason that there are things you must continue to put in place to ensure the ever-burning of the fire.

Therefore, we are going to look into these practicalities of maintaining or ensuring that the Spirit is not quenched. So in this last section, I'm going to lead you once again into the practical ways of keeping the divine Presence in your life so that you will always experience victory and divine security as you go about your day to day activities to the glory of Christ.

Firstly, to keep the Spirit burning, you must always walk in the consciousness of the divine Presence of the Spirit of God, *Ruach HaKodesh*, in your life. For the Scripture says: "**Know ye not that ye are the temple of God, and that the Spirit of God dwelleth in you?**" (1 Corinthians 3:16). You must know and understand that you, as a son or daughter of God in Christ, that you are a carrier of God's Presence. That means when you show up, God's Presence shows up, and wherever you are God's Presence is there also. "*And what agreement hath the temple of God with idols? **for ye are the temple of the living God**; as God hath said, **I will dwell in them, and walk in them; and I will be their God, and they shall be my people**. Wherefore come out from among them, and be ye separate, saith the Lord, and touch not the unclean thing; and I will receive you. And will be a Father unto you, and ye shall be my sons and daughters, saith the Lord Almighty*". (2 Corinthians 6:16-18).

Jesus said to Philip: ".*Have I been with you for*

so long a time, and you do not know Me yet, Philip, nor recognize clearly who I am? **Anyone who has seen Me has seen the Father.** *How can you say, 'Show us the Father?"* (John 14:9 AMP). Did you get that? You are in Christ, and anyone who has seen Christ has seen the Father, which means anyone who sees you have seen the Father also because you are in Christ. Look at the next verse: *"Do you not believe that I am in the Father, and the Father is in Me? The words I say to you I do not say on My own initiative or authority,* **but the Father, abiding continually in Me,** *does His works [His attesting miracles and acts of power]".* (John 14:10. AMP). You must always walk in this mindset that you are dwelling in the secret place of the Most High and that you are surrounded by the consuming fire of the everlasting burnings. That is what John meant when he said: "Ye are of God, little children, and have overcome them: because **greater is he that is in you than he that is in the world."** (1 John 4:4).

You must believe that you are a carrier of God's Presence. You must believe that you are dwelling in the secret place of the Most High and that you are abiding under the shadow of the Almighty. You must let it establish in the spirit of your mind that you are living in the very Presence of the Omnipresent and that nothing negative can touch you or anything that concerns you. The Scripture says that the just shall live by faith. (See Hebrews 10:38, and Habakkuk 2:4). And you are the righteousness of God in Christ, (See 2 Corinthians 5:21). Therefore, you must live by faith, which is the foundation of your Christian walk and your obedience to Scriptures. You must release your faith because your actions of faith are the evidence that you believe, for, without faith (actions), no one can please God. (See Hebrews 11:6).

Some people claim that they believe, but by their actions, we know that they don't believe because you cannot believe and not act in the manner conforming to that which you believe. That is what James meant when he said: *show me your faith without your actions, and I will show you my faith by my actions.* (See James 2:18). That Scripture is a challenge, so release your faith. Act accordingly, and be bold, be daring and be audacious, that is the spirit of faith.

Your act of faith is the confirmation that you believe, and that confirmation is what heaven is waiting to see in you. Divine intervention is based on your act of faith. Do you know that Jesus expected His disciples to speak to the windstorm when He was asleep in the boat in Matthew 8:24-27? Because after they woke Him up and before He rebuked the storm by His words, He said to His disciples: *"Why are you fearful,* **O you men of little faith.***"* In other words, they could have spoken to the windstorm the same way Jesus did, and the storm would have obeyed them the same way it obeyed Jesus. Your act of faith in response to the Rhema-Word of God in your spirit in any given circumstance is what produces the miraculous.

Elisha understood this principle of faith. In 2 Kings chapter two, when his master and father in the Lord, Elijah was about to be taken to heaven, they journeyed to Gilgal and from Gilgal to Bethel and then to Jericho. As they journeyed, the Scripture says that *"Elijah took his mantle, and wrapped it together, and smote the waters, and they were divided hither and thither so that the two of them crossed over on dry ground."* (2 kings 2:8). Don't forget that Elisha was right beside Elijah when he smote the waters with his mantle. Now after Elijah has been taken to heaven by a chariot of fire and horses of fire and Elisha has also received the mantle of Elijah that fell from him as he was taken up, on his way back, Elisha did the same thing Elijah did. *"And he took the mantle of Elijah that fell from him, and smote the waters, and said, Where is the Lord God of Elijah? (acknowledgment of power source) and when he also had smitten the waters, they parted hither and thither: and Elisha went over"*. (2 Kings 2:14). The river Jordan parted hither and thither for Elisha the same way it did for Elijah, and that was because Elisha confirmed that he believed in the God of Elijah by his actions of faith. You must always release your faith in actions. That is what produces the miraculous in your life. That is what James the Apostle meant when he said: *"But be ye doers of the word, and not hearers only, deceiving your own selves."* (James 1:22). You see, when you don't act in faith, you deceive yourself, which means that you deny yourself the miraculous that comes by faith.

Be a man or a woman of faith. Always meditate and speak the word of God. And as God quickens a specific Rhema into your spirit in a particular situation, act on that Rhema in faith, and you will always experience the miraculous like never before. The Light of God is shining in you. The power of the Spirit is at work in your life. You can't fail. You can't be defeated or manipulated. You can't be sick, no, it's not possible. You are a child of God, which means that you are a god. The ability of God in you is unlimited and immeasurable. You are the best of the best of your kind. He made you in His image and likeness, and He gave you all power and authority to have dominion over the whole earth for His glory. Let this reality of your divine identity form your mentality. Immerse yourself deeply into these truths and let them become your frame of mind beginning from this minute.

Secondly, to ensure that the fire of the Spirit is ever burning in your life, which guarantees your divine security on every side, you must master the art of singing praises to the name of the Lord. Each time you offer praises to the Lord with gratitude and love in your heart for Him, you increase the fire of the everlasting burnings in your life. Waking up early morning and taking some time to sing praises to the Lord is a very powerful way of starting your day. Get some anointed gospel songs and put it on as you wake up so that your soul can be lifted up to God in praise and worship before starting your day.

In my bedroom, I always make sure an anointed song is playing even before going to bed, and then when I wake up in the early morning hours to pray, my soul will just flow with the songs in praise and worship to the Lord, and my day is always great and miraculous. *"Let the people praise thee, O God; let all the people praise thee. Then shall the earth yield her increase; and **God, even our own God, shall bless us. God shall bless us,** and all the ends of the earth shall fear him"*. (Psalm 67:5-7). Singing praises to the Lord in the early morning hours is one of the secrets of obtaining victory daily, but a lot of Christians don't know this. Once they wake up, take a shower, they just get dressed and off for the day. That's a very wrong way to start your day as a Christian. The Scripture says: *"Blessed be the Lord, who **daily loadeth us with benefits,** even the God of our salvation."* (Psalm 68:19).

To bless the Lord is to sing praises to His name. When you wake up early morning and, first of all, lift up your soul in praise and worship to God, you increase His Presence in your life, and your day is blessed. Look at another secret of David: "*In the morning, O Lord, You will hear my voice; In the morning, I will prepare [a prayer and a sacrifice] for You and watch and wait [for You to speak to my heart].*" (Psalm 5:3. AMP). That's it. After praying and offering sacrifices of praise to God in the early morning hours of the day, you will not only have a great day; He will also speak to your heart with a divine revelation for more blessing upon your life. When you worship God in a high spirit praises, you are expressing your love and gratitude towards Him for all His goodness, mercy, and grace towards you and your household.

In 2 Chronicles 20:1-30, we saw a situation where the only solution was to sing praises to the Lord. The children of Moab and the children of Ammon ganged up together with allies to attack Judah and Jerusalem. Then the news was brought to the king Jehoshaphat, who, upon hearing the news, went and sought God with all the people. By seeking God, Jehoshaphat was inspired by divine revelation on how to obtain the desired victory:

*"And they rose **early in the morning**, and went forth into the wilderness of Tekoa: and as they went forth, Jehoshaphat stood and said, Hear me, O Judah, and ye inhabitants of Jerusalem; Believe in the Lord your God, so shall ye be established; believe his prophets, so shall ye prosper.*

*And when he had consulted with the people, **he appointed singers unto the Lord**, and that **should praise** the beauty of holiness, as they went out before the army, and to say, Praise the Lord; for his mercy endureth for ever.*

And when they began to sing and to praise, the Lord set ambushments against the children of Ammon, Moab, and mount Seir, which were come against Judah; and they were smitten.

For the children of Ammon and Moab stood up against the inhabitants of mount Seir, utterly to slay and destroy them: and when they had made an end of the inhabitants of Seir, every one helped to destroy another". (2 Chronicles 20:20-23).

Anytime you lift up your soul in singing praises and worship to God, you experience divine intervention, which is divine security. He goes before you and destroys every obstacle even before you know. That is the reason manifold miracles take place whenever Christians gather together in singing praises and worship to God. *"But thou art holy, O thou that inhabitest (lives in) the praises of His people."* (Psalm 22:3) Worshiping the Lord with praises in high spirit intensifies the miraculous workings of His Presence in your life, and it produces manifold blessings in your favor. Therefore always engage in singing praises to the Lord in the early morning hours of the day and watch mountains of obstacles as they crumble and become plain before you. (See Zechariah 4:7).

Thirdly, to maintain and to continually intensify the Presence of God in your life, you must constantly and continuously be listening to inspired messages of the gospel of Christ. This is very important, especially if you are someone who gets very busy at the office during the day. Get the messages of great men and women of God on CDs, DVDs, and tapes, even the Audiobooks, and listen as you do your work in the office. When the apostle Paul said: "*Quench not the Spirit,*" he quickly added, "despise not prophesying," which means; *do not despise inspired messages.* (See 1 Thessalonians 5:19-20). Most of our daily activities are with our hands, not with our ears, except when on phone calls. So as you are busy working, you are being inspired by the messages as they play.

Even in your car, as you drive from home to the office and so forth, make sure messages are playing so that you can get inspired as you drive. You can as well download them on your mobile device and listen to them while on the bus, train, tram, or metro, and also when you are traveling on a flight. Wherever you are, make sure you are listening to inspired messages of God's Word. Moses understood this very well when said: "*And these words, which I command thee this day, shall be in thine heart: And thou shalt teach them diligently unto thy children, and shalt talk of them when thou sittest in thine house, and when thou walkest by the way, and when thou liest down, and when thou risest up. And thou shalt bind them for a sign upon thine hand, and they shall be as frontlets between thine eyes. And thou shalt write them upon the posts of thy house, and on thy gates*". (Deuteronomy 6:6-9).

You must master the art of utilizing every opportunity in planting the seed of God's Word into your heart. Don't forget: *in the Word is the seed of God's blessing.* You must be doing this consistently and never become tired or allow yourself to become familiar with the Word. That is very important because once you become familiar with the Word, the next thing is that you start losing your passion, the fire of the Spirit will begin to go out, and we are told never to allow the fire to go out; "*The fire on the altar shall be kept burning;* **it shall not [be allowed to] go out.** *The priest shall burn wood on it every morning, and he shall arrange the burnt offering on it and offer the fat portions of the peace offerings up in smoke on it. The fire shall be burning continually on the altar;* **it shall not [be allowed to] go out**". (Leviticus 6:12-13. AMP). It shall not be allowed to go out is said in verse 12 and repeated again in verse 13, which shows how important it is to keep the fire burning.

How do you keep the fire burning? He told you in verse 12; *"The priest shall burn wood on it every morning"* and who is the priest? You are. *"You (Christ) have made them to be a kingdom [of royal subjects] and **priests to our God**, and they will reign on the earth."* (Revelation 5:10. AMP). Now you see that you are the priest, and you shall burn wood in the fire every morning. Ok, now, what is the wood? The wood is the Word of God, as you keep listening to the Word and study the Scriptures every morning as you pray and sing praise to God before starting your day, you are burning the wood, and the fire in you is ever going up. Even if it's just thirty minutes devotion every morning before starting your day, that is great, and you will be amazed how sweet your day will be. Without the wood, the fire will go out, for *"Where no wood is, there the fire goeth out"* (See Proverbs 26:20). Therefore, you must always ensure that the fire of the Spirit, which is the Presence of God in your life, is ever burning by adding more wood (the Word) on the fire every morning.

Finally, to keep the fire of the Spirit burning, you must master the art of fasting with prayer. As you sing and pray every day, study your Bible every day, and listen to inspired messages every day, don't let a whole month pass by without taking some days to go into fasting and prayer. This is very important because fasting and prayer has a lot to do with divine revelations by which you prosper, and divine Presence, by which you walk in divine security. Fasting is a spiritual exercise you must always engage in, at least once in every month. Fasting is a divine prescription from the Lord to keep you in a constant vibrant spiritual and physical health and attuned to Him. *"Then shall thy **light** (divine revelation) break forth as the morning, and thine **health** (vibrant health) shall spring forth speedily: and thy righteousness (divine peace and prosperity) shall go before thee; the **glory** (divine presence) of the Lord shall be thy reward (divine security)."* (Isaiah 58:8).

You see that fasting covers every area of your life, from divine revelation to vibrant health, and then to divine peace and prosperity and then to divine Presence, which automatically guarantees divine security. Fasting is also a spiritual exercise through which you obtain speedy answers to your prayers. *"Then shalt thou call, and the **Lord shall answer**; thou shalt cry, and he shall say, **Here I am**."* (Isaiah 58:9). Fasting also increases the light of God in you as you reach out to help those who are in need. *"For if thou draw out thy soul to the hungry, and satisfy the afflicted soul; **then shall thy light rise in obscurity, and thy darkness be as the noonday**."* (Isaiah 58:10).

When you fast often, you enjoy divine direction continually, which means that you will always be divinely guided in everything you do and everywhere you go. Not only that, but you will also experience an overabundance of divine provisions on every side. Everything around and about you will be flourishing limitlessly. *"The Lord shall guide thee continually, and satisfy thy soul in drought, and make fat thy bones: and thou shalt be like a watered garden, and like a spring of water, whose waters fail not."* (Isaiah 58:11). As a Christian, you are required to fast often. Jesus said: *"Moreover **when ye fast**, be not, as the hypocrites, of a sad countenance: for they disfigure their faces, that they may appear unto men to fast. Ver-*

ily I say unto you, They have their reward. But thou, when thou fastest, anoint thine head, and wash thy face; That thou appear not unto men to fast, but unto thy Father which is in secret: and thy Father, which seeth in secret, shall reward thee openly". (Matthew 6:16-18). Did you notice He said *when you fast*, not if you fast? That means fasting is a command from the Lord. It's an exercise you cannot do without. When you fast often, your spiritual sensitivity is sharpened, and you can rightly discern things quickly without guessing. When you fast, you become acquainted and attuned with the voice of God in your spirit. Fasting launches you into the realm of unlimited possibilities where you command things and they answer at the instance of your command.

I take two days in every week to seek the Lord in fasting and prayer, and sometimes I take it up to ten to fourteen days in each month, just to enjoy the Presence of the Lord and hear what He has to tell me or show me. Most of the revelations I have encountered was during a fast, and I can tell you, it's awesome. Fasting gives you unusual access to divine mysteries. It increases your faith and reinforces your spiritual stamina.

When you fast often, the strength of your flesh is weakened and subdued, and your spirit rises to dominance. Fasting dissipates tensions and eradicates fear out of your mind. You must also understand that fasting intensifies prayers; in fact, the essence of fasting is to amplify the efficacy of your prayer. That is why you can't fast without praying, but you can pray without fasting. Fasting without prayer becomes a mere hunger strike, and you don't want to waste your time and energy on a fruitless exercise. So you must always pray during fasting. No matter how busy you are, you can always pause and speak to the Lord in prayer. You must also understand that both fasting and prayer is for the glory of God. It's a *secret* spiritual exercise that you engage in from time to time without appearing to people to be fasting or praying. It's not something you announce to family, friends, and colleagues at work or your business place.

There is a difference between *proclaimed* fasting and *private* fasting. A proclaimed fasting is when a group of individuals come together in one mind to seek the Lord in fasting and prayer over a common goal. Like in our church, we do proclaim a fast from time to time, and everyone will fast and pray to the Lord for the church, and that also can be personal after the church has proclaimed it. A private fast, on the other hand, is when you are led by the Spirit to go on a fast, or you just decide to seek the Lord in fasting and prayer for your personal goal.

When I fast, I don't pre-announce it even to my wife and children. By the time I skip meals for a whole day or two, my wife will automatically get the message that I'm waiting on the Lord, and so as my children. The same way, when my wife skips meals for a whole day, I will just know that she is fasting. Fasting and prayer is a secret activity that you engage in for God's glory. When fasting, take a shower often, and wash your mouth often using mouth wash. Always dress well so that people won't start asking you if you are fasting. That is what Jesus meant when He said: *"But thou, when thou fastest, anoint thine head, and wash thy face;* **That thou appear not unto men to fast, but unto thy Father**

which is in secret: *and thy Father, which seeth in secret, shall reward thee openly.*" (Matthew 6:17-18). That's it. When it comes to fasting and prayer, be secretive about it, and your Father, which *sees in secret*, will reward you openly, meaning that your blessing for fasting will not be denied; instead, it will come to the attention of all.

Fasting for only twelve hours a day, which is the general six to six fasting, and then eating your regular favorite meal in the evening is not really intense fasting. But you can achieve something if the twelve hours are invested in prayers and the study of scriptures. Intense fasting that works wonders involves going for at least three days without food and water and coupled with intense prayer and the study of scriptures together with a great book that talks about the issue for which you are fasting. During such fasting, you must take only warm water if you have to be busy during the day. Any other time must be invested in praying and studying the Scriptures because that is what provokes the outbreak of divine revelation. At the end of the fast, which is the morning of the fourth day, you must break the fast with a low quantity of fresh fruits and green vegetable salad. You must continue with the fresh fruits and green vegetable salad for two days before you gradually resume your regular meal. The reason is that your entire body system went through cleansing during the fast, and so your stomach, which has hibernated during the fast, will need almost the same days of the fast to be ready for your regular meals again. This cleansing that your body undergoes during fasting is the reason why you feel very much alive and healthy after the fast, both physically and spiritually.

As we approach the conclusion of this book, I want you to understand that as you study the Scriptures and pray, both during and after fasting, speak the words of God. Let the words of Christ determine your daily conversation. Speak faith at all times. Speak positive and life-giving words. Don't let anything contrary to your expectations come out of your mouth. Focus your mind always on the positive. Build up your mind on Scriptures. Let the words of Christ *tabernacle* in you in abundance and in all wisdom and spiritual understanding. With all diligence, guard your heart and mind against negativity, for out of your heart and mind comes the issues of life. (See Proverbs 4:23).

The knowledge of wisdom is the knowledge of the Holy. It abhors and detests negativity and falsehood. God is light, and in Him, there is no darkness at all. (See 1 John 1:5). He is perfect in knowledge, wonderful in counsel, and *excellent in working*. (See Isaiah 28:29).

Four

Conclusion

Conclusion

*"My son, eat thou honey, because it is good; and the honeycomb, which is sweet to thy taste: So shall **the knowledge of wisdom** be unto thy soul: when thou hast found it, then there shall be a reward, and thy expectation shall not be cut off". (Proverbs 24:13-14).*

The keys to the knowledge of wisdom have just been delivered into your hands via this book. Your empowerment to walking in the light of divine peace, prosperity, and security has just begun.

An idea followed by action is what rules the world. Therefore, as you begin to operate by the knowledge of wisdom as detailed in this book, your rewards of blessing will abound in exceeding measure, and your expectations, which shall never be cut off, will exceed your wildest imagination.

You are the only *you* that God has created. You are the best of the best of your kind. No one is like you, and no one will ever be like you. You are unique and peculiar, endowed with limitless power and tremendous light. Now, *go and shine!*

ABOUT THE AUTHOR

JEROHAM C. IBEH is the author of The Seven Principles, The Wisdom for Mighty Works, and Mastering the Forces of Success. He is also the founder and senior pastor of The Greater Success House of God, a Christian Church organization that focuses on the teachings of Biblical Applications for Prosperous and Successful Living, which includes The Greater Success Youth Convention, an annual youth empowerment program that focuses on empowering youths with Biblical revelations for the maximization of their potentials and fulfillment of their great destinies. Having studied Christian Theology, Christian Leadership and Youth Ministry at the Christian Leaders Institute in Spring Lake, Michigan USA, Jeroham C. Ibeh has passionately dedicated his life to teaching and impacting lives globally with the teachings on Biblical Application for Successful Living, which he termed "The Knowledge of the Truth." He lives in Nigeria with his wife and children.

By Jeroham C. Ibeh

- The Wisdom For Might Works

- The Seven Principles

- Mastering The Forces Of Success

- The Knowledge of Wisdom

Gushing Stream Publications Ltd

Lagos - Nigeria

Email: gushingstreampublications@gmail.com

Follow us on Facebook and Instagram to stay up to date on your favorite books and daily motivational and inspirational quotes from our authors.

facebook.com/GushingStream   **instagram.com/GushingStream**

www.ingramcontent.com/pod-product-compliance
Lightning Source LLC
La Vergne TN
LVHW091712190726
843493LV00001B/264